WITHDRAWN

Access Services

SPEC KITS

Supporting Effective Library Management for Over Twenty Years

Committed to assisting research and academic libraries in the continuous improvement of management systems, OLMS has worked since 1970 to gather and disseminate the best practices for library needs. As part of its committment, OLMS maintains an active publications program best known for its SPEC Kits. Through the OLMS Collaborative Research/Writing Program, librarians work with ARL staff to design SPEC surveys and write publications. Originally established as an information source for ARL member libraries, the SPEC series has grown to serve the needs of the library community worldwide.

What are SPEC Kits?

Published six times per year, SPEC Kits contain the most valuable, up-to-date information on the latest issues of concern to libraries and librarians today. They are the result of a systematic survey of ARL member libraries on a particular topic related to current practice in the field. Each SPEC Kit contains an executive summary of the survey results (previously printed as the SPEC Flyer); survey questions with tallies and selected comments; the best representative documents from survey participants, such as policies, procedures, handbooks, guidelines, websites, records, brochures, and statements; and a selected reading list—both in print and online sources—containing the most current literature available on the topic for further study.

Subscribe to SPEC Kits

Subscribers tell us that the information contained in SPEC Kits is valuable to a variety of users, both inside and outside the library. SPEC Kit purchasers use the documentation found in SPEC Kits as a point of departure for research and problem solving because they lend immediate authority to proposals and set standards for designing programs or writing procedure statements. SPEC Kits also function as an important reference tool for library administrators, staff, students, and professionals in allied disciplines who may not have access to this kind of information.

SPEC Kits can be ordered directly from the ARL Publications Distribution Center. To order, call **(301) 362-8196**, fax **(301) 206-9789**, e-mail **pubs@arl.org**, or go to **http://www.arl.org/pubscat/**.

Information on SPEC Kits and other OLMS products and services can be found on the ARL Web site at **http://www.arl.org/olms/infosvcs.html**. The Web site for the SPEC survey program is **http://www.arl.org/spec/**. The executive summary or flyer for each kit after December 1993 can be accessed free of charge at the SPEC survey Web site.

SPEC Kit 290

Access Services
November 2005

Trevor A. Dawes

Circulation Services Director

Princeton University

Kimberly Burke Sweetman

Head, Access Services

New York University

Catherine Von Elm

Head of Circulation, Current Periodicals, and Microforms

University of Pennsylvania

ASSOCIATION OF RESEARCH LIBRARIES

OFFICE OF LEADERSHIP AND
MANAGEMENT SERVICES

Series Editor: Lee Anne George

SPEC Kits are published by the

Association of Research Libraries
Office of Leadership and Management Services
21 Dupont Circle, NW, Suite 800
Washington, D.C. 20036-1118
(202) 296-2296 Fax (202) 872-0884
http://www.arl.org/olms/infosvcs.html
pubs@arl.org

ISSN 0160 3582

ISBN 1-59407-698-7

EAN 9781594076985

SPEC
Kit 290

Access Services

November 2005

SURVEY RESULTS

Executive Summary..11

Survey Questions and Responses..15

Responding Institutions 40

REPRESENTATIVE DOCUMENTS

Organization Charts
Arizona State University
    Access Services...44
University of California, Davis
    General Library Organization Chart...45
    Access Services Department...46
University of California, Irvine
    UCIrvine/Libraries..47
    Public Services..48
University of California, Santa Barbara
    Davidson Library Organization Chart...49
    Access Services...50
University of Connecticut
    Access Services...51
University of Florida
    Organization Chart...52
Florida State University
    Academic Affairs. University Libraries. Administration....................................53
    Academic Affairs. University Libraries. Public Services. Reference/Circulation/Gov Documents 54
University of Illinois at Chicago
    Library Users (patrons, clients, customers)..55

University of Iowa

    The University of Iowa Libraries. Organization Chart...56

Iowa State University

    Organization Chart. Iowa State University Library 57

University of Miami

    Otto G. Richter Library. Access & Delivery Services Organization Chart..................................58

University of Minnesota

    Library Access Services..59

University of Missouri

    MU Libraries..60

University of North Carolina at Chapel Hill

    University Library 61

North Carolina State University

    North Carolina State University Libraries Organizational Chart...62

    Access and Delivery Services...63

Northwestern University

    Library Administration. Organization Chart...64

University of Oklahoma

    Organization Chart. University Libraries...65

Pennsylvania State University

    University Libraries. Organization Chart...66

    Access Services 67

Princeton University

    Organization Chart. Princeton University Library 68

    Technical Services Department...69

Purdue University

    Purdue University Libraries 70

    Purdue University Libraries. Access Services Organization 71

Temple University

    Plan of Library Organization...72

University of Tennessee

    University of Tennessee Libraries..73

University of Utah

    J. Willard Marriott Library..74

Virginia Tech

    Virginia Tech University Libraries..75

University of Washington

    Research and Instructional Services...76

Washington University in St. Louis

    WU Libraries & Information Technology Organization Chart..77

University of Waterloo

    Circulation Services..78

Circulation/Access Services Mission Statements

Brigham Young University
Circulation. Mission 80
University of California, Davis
Access Services Department. Mission and Goals..81
University of Connecticut
Access Services. Mission Statement 83
University of Minnesota
Information Access & Delivery Services. Mission, Vision, Values...................................84
University of Oklahoma
Access Services 85
Princeton University
Circulation Division. About the Circulation Services Division 86
Tulane University
Access Services & Circulation..87
University of Utah
Access Services 88

Circulation/Access Services Home Pages

University of California, Santa Barbara
Access Services 90
Indiana University Bloomington
Customer and Access Services 91
University of Iowa
Access Services 92
University of North Carolina at Chapel Hill
Davis Circulation-Home Page..93
University of Oregon
Knight Library Access Services Department...94
University of Tennessee
Access and Delivery Services...95
Washington State University
Access Services 96
University of Waterloo
Circulation Services...98

Job Descriptions

Arizona State University
Position Description. Head, Access Services and Interlibrary Loan................................100

University of California, Davis
    Statement of Primary Responsibilities. Head, Access Services Dept...............................103
University of California, Santa Barbara
    Statement of Duties and Responsibilities. Head of Access Services...............................105
University of Chicago
    Assistant Director, Access & Facilities...106
University of Connecticut
    Job Description. Director of Library Access Services 108
George Washington University
    Head, Circulation/Reserves Department..111
North Carolina State University
    Head, Access and Delivery Services..113
University of Oklahoma
    Head, Access Services 114
Pennsylvania State University
    Statement of Core Responsibilities (Head of Access Services).................................115
Princeton University
    Circulation Services Director 116
Purdue University
    Head, Access Services 118
University of Utah
    Head of Circulation and Interlibrary Loans...119
Virginia Tech
    Unit Head, Circulation/Reserve/Storage 121
University of Washington
    Coordinator for Access Services 124
Washington University in St. Louis
    Head of Access...126

SELECTED RESOURCES

Journal Articles...129
Additional Circulation/Access Services Web Sites 129
Library Services Web Sites 130

SURVEY RESULTS

EXECUTIVE SUMMARY

Introduction

In 1991, SPEC Kit 179 *Access Services: Organization and Management* documented the emergence of a new trend in ARL member libraries. Over the course of a decade, a variety of services related to providing access to library resources were being brought under one administrative umbrella. That department was typically called "Circulation," though a growing number of libraries began to use the term "Access Services."

In the spring of 2005, this follow-up survey was conducted with the intent of tracking developments and trends in access services since 1995. Seventy-seven of the 123 ARL member libraries (63%) responded to the survey, indicating an ongoing interest in both the topic of access services and the functions of access services departments. The survey results presented here also show a steady evolution in department name from circulation to access services and an increasing relevance of this depatment's functions to library users.

Background

All but three of the seventy-seven libraries responding to the current survey have a discreet department that has primary responsibility for circulation and other activities related to accessing collections. Sixty-three of these departments have either the word "circulation" or "access" in their name. The decade between 1995 and 2005 saw a marked decrease in the number of departments identified solely as "Circulation," though: 39% of

the respondents used that name in 1995 compared to only 14% in 2005. The survey responses indicate that at least eight libraries changed the department name to "Access Services" in each five-year period between 1991 and 2005; the single largest increase was during the period 1996 to 2000, when fifteen institutions changed names. In addition to the increasingly popular "Access Services," other names for these departments include "Borrower Services," "Collection Services," and "Resource Support Services."

Changes in Department Activities

While there is no single prototype for the range of services provided by these departments, there is a set of five services that has remained core under the circulation/access umbrella from 1991 to 1995 to 2005: circulation; stacks maintenance and shelving; billing; entry/exit control; and reserve services, both print and electronic. A smaller but consistent number of circulation/access services departments have also had responsibility for retrieval from off-site shelving, study-carrel registration, and library security since 1995.

Between 1995 and 2005, a growing number of circulation/access services departments absorbed other traditional library units and took on responsibility for new services. Some of these changes, such as the increase in circulation/access services departments that have responsibility for current periodicals (+19%), microforms (+28%), the information desk (+38%), and interlibrary loan (+39%)

are likely the result of organizational restructuring. The increase in the number of these departments offering on-campus document delivery (+100%), circulation of laptops (+200%), and electronic reserves (+269%) is certainly attributable to the wider adoption of new services made possible, in part, by new technology. It also indicates that circulation/access services departments are responding to the demands of students and faculty in the "we want it wherever we are" environment and that libraries have become more service oriented as a whole.

In addition to these activities, a number of respondents reported an array of other offerings such as services for users with disabilities, catalog maintenance, computer lab maintenance, shipping and receiving, copyright clearance, in-house printing, and copy card sales, to name a few. Only a handful of respondents reported handing off an activity to another department in the past ten years; these include small declines in the number of circulation/access services departments that now have responsibility for entry/exit control, study-carrel registration, photocopy services, preservation, lockers, and distance learning.

As units were combined and services added, service points were consolidated. Forty-two respondents reported that multiple services were offered from 55 separate service desks in 1995. These were most often either the former circulation desk, reserves desk, or reserves/current periodicals desk. Fifty-four respondents reported that there were 81 consolidated service points by 2005. Between 1995 and 2005, eight respondents reported that single-service desks merged to form multi-service desks and at least twelve others reported that brand new multi-service desks were created. At eight of the responding libraries multi-service desks split to provide different combinations of services; in two cases some services left the access services department. Thirty-six combined desks added services such as interlibrary loan/document delivery, media, laptop circulation, and other responsibilities; only three dropped any services. Service-desk offerings remained the same from 1995 to 2005 at nineteen libraries.

On average, staffed service-desk hours increased across the board between 1995 and 2005. At most of the responding libraries any increase (or decrease) was just a few hours per week. The most dramatic increases were reported by a handful of libraries that have combined multiple services at one desk and staffed it all (or most of) the hours the building is open. For example, one library increased service-desk hours from 82 per week to 160 per week. Other large jumps were from 101 to 133, 102 to 154, 105 to 133, and 107 to 146 hours per week.

Automation has had a significant impact on the staff workflow in circulation/access services departments over the past decade. With the exception of entry/exit control and accounting, which were fairly well automated by 1995, and stacks maintenance, which remains fairly unautomated, survey respondents reported increases of between 100% and over 600% in the automation of every staff activity. The substantial increase in the automation of some processes, such as notices, billing, bindery, and the submission and management of interlibrary loan requests (109%, 125%, 135%, and 158% respectively), is probably a reflection of the normal rate of development and adoption of suitable software. The jump in automation of offsite storage retrieval requests (420%), on the other hand, is more likely attributable to the increase in the number of libraries that rely on storage facilities to manage overcrowded stacks and maintain access to low-use items than it is to the fact that the requests themselves are automated.

Between 1995 and 2005, library users also benefited from an increase in automation. The majority of respondents now offer online "do-it-yourself" renewals, ILL requesting, storage-retrieval requesting, and document delivery. Forty-one percent offer self-service circulation. Library users may also make multimedia reservations, register for study carrels, submit materials for reserves, and place holds and recalls online.

Staffing and Reporting Relationships

Though about half of the respondents reported that the supervisor of the circulation/access services department has a title of Head of Access Services or Head of Circulation Services, the specific titles vary widely. Nonetheless, the titles and the reporting relationships indicate that these individuals hold high-level management positions. Two-thirds report to an assistant or associate dean or director in their libraries; 21% report to a library dean or director; 13% report to the head of a division or a branch library.

Roughly equal numbers of respondents reported that the number of positions in the circulation/access services department increased, decreased, and stayed the same between 1995 and 2005. Slightly more respondents reported an increase in the number of student assistants and a decrease in the number of support staff. Librarian and other professional positions were more likely to stay the same. On average, there are two librarians and two and a half other professionals in each department. The bulk of the department is made up of support staff and student assistants, about 23 of each.

As the functions associated with circulation/access services departments have increased, become more automated, and arguably more complex, so has the need for staff to become versed in a greater variety of functions. With the steady-state or decline in staffing, the amount of cross-training of staff has increased: 82% of respondents indicated that staff were trained to perform at least two functions in 2005, as compared with only 34% in 1995. Similarly, the survey results show a decrease in specialization from 1995 (79%) to 2005 (36%). At the same time, the respondents' comments make clear that even today some staff focus on specialized areas of expertise while others are generalists.

Budget

Half of the circulation/access services departments have a distinct operating budget and half do not. All but one of the operating budgets covers student wages. The majority of these budgets include funds for salaries, office supplies and equipment, and printing or copying. Other budget categories include equipment rental and repair, telecommunications, postage, travel and training support, and contracts. All but a few of the department heads manage the wage budget and many manage supplies. Only about a quarter manage equipment, personnel, or other budget categories. Budgets range from $66,000 to $4,000,000 with an average of $668,220. There seems to be a correlation between the very highest budget levels and the number of support staff, but that does not hold true for the lower budgets.

Service Evaluation

The responding libraries use a variety of techniques to evaluate the effectiveness of circulation and access services. Almost all of them track the number of circulation transactions and most track the use of other services. Seventy percent of respondents have used the LibQUAL+™ survey to solicit user satisfaction feedback on these services. Other techniques for gathering user feedback include focus groups, interviews of both internal and external users, comment cards and suggestion boxes, and usability studies, among others.

Conclusion

The 1991 SPEC survey defined access services as the department responsible for "physical access to library collections." The operation of current access services departments has evolved, transforming existing services and adding new ones—primarily due to technological innovations and to the priority placed on meeting user demand for delivery of services and resources. While still the locus for physical access to print collections (circulation, stacks and storage maintenance, reserves), access services is expanding its mission to include not only *access* to physical and electronic collections, but also *delivery* of these resources, regardless of whether they are licensed, or held locally, remotely, or consortially. This trend was brought about partly by the evolving nature of information storage and the access-vs-ownership library model, and partly by the advances in technology that streamlined the requesting process for users and facilitated request management by staff.

Access services departments have both responded to and transformed the ways users identify, request, and receive resources remotely and have also maintained the competing priority of assisting users in the library. Combining service points, expanding hours of service, and cross-training staff have enabled access services departments to broaden the array of services provided, and of physical items circulated, such as videos and laptop computers.

As emerging technology and the trend toward automation continues to have an impact on how users interact with the library, and on the library's ability to provide access to resources, access services departments will continue to evolve by combining service points and previously discreet departments; adjusting hours of service and staffing; and constantly revising procedures to better serve users.

SURVEY QUESTIONS and RESPONSES

The SPEC survey on Access Services was designed by Trevor A. Dawes, Circulation Services Director, Princeton University; Kimberly Burke Sweetman, Head, Access Services, New York University; and Catherine Von Elm, Head of Circulation, Current Periodicals, and Microforms, University of Pennsylvania. These results are based on data submitted by 77 of the 123 ARL member libraries (63%) by the deadline of March 21, 2005. The survey's introductory text and questions are reproduced below, followed by the response data and selected comments from the respondents.

The term access services first emerged as a library department name in the 1980s. In 1991, SPEC Kit 179 Access Services: Organization and Management explored the access services department trend. At that time access services units were evolving from primarily covering circulation to encompassing core activities such as interlibrary loan, reserves, and stacks management, among others. The range of activities and the channels of service delivery in access services have continued to change since 1991. Reserves are now made available electronically; renewals, holds, and check-outs are increasingly unmediated; libraries have begun lending laptop computers and videos in addition to traditional materials; procedures have been established for the retrieval of materials from storage facilities; and direct consortial borrowing and desktop document delivery have expanded the range of resources readily available to users.

Access services staff responsibilities have likewise changed. These staff frequently administer the library's confidentiality policies and procedures—made more complex in an age of wireless access to Internet resources—and manage service points that are staffed days, evenings, and weekends by a combination of professionals, paraprofessionals, and student assistants. Issues of customer service, building access, and emergency facilities responses frequently fall within the purview of access services departments. A central challenge to all access services staff is maintaining high levels of service while revising existing procedures and policies to keep pace with user demand, technological innovations, and developments in information storage, access, and retrieval.

This survey is designed to investigate the continued evolution of access services in ARL member libraries and identify changes in the range of services, organizational structure, staffing levels, and budget since 1991. It will also identify changes anticipated in the near future. The results will provide a snapshot of access services departments in research libraries at the beginning of the 21st century.

BACKGROUND

1. Does your library have a department that has primary responsibility for circulation and other activities related to accessing collections, such as reserves, stacks maintenance, interlibrary loan, etc.? N=77

Yes	74	96%	Please complete the survey.
No	3	4%	Please submit the survey now.

2. Please indicate the name of that department today and what it was called in 1995. If there are plans to change the name in the near future, indicate the new department name. N=71

	1995	2005	Near Future
Access	28	39	2
Circulation	27	10	—
Other	15	22	3

Other Names in 1995

Circulation/Reserves Department

Circulation + other individual units: Reserves, ILL

Circulation and Interlibrary Loan and Extension Library

Circulation Department and another department called IRRC/ILL and another department within undergraduate library called Reserves

Circulation, Interlibrary Loan, and Facilities

Collection Management Division

CMD/Loan

General Services

Humanities and History Division

Information Access

Information Access and Delivery Services Team

Stack Maintenance and Delivery

User Services

Other Names in 2005

Access & Branch Services

Access & Delivery Services

Access & Facilities Services

Access Services/Interlibrary Loan

Borrower Services

Circulation & Interlibrary Services

Circulation and Media Services

Circulation/Reserves Department

Circulation Department and another department called IRRC/ILL and another department within undergraduate library called Media/Reserves

Circulation/Interlibrary Loan

Circulation/Reserve/Document Delivery Department

Collection Services

Customer and Access Services

Information Access

Information Access and Delivery Services Team

Onsite Access Services

Resource Support Services

Future Names

From:	To:
Access Services	Access and Preservation Services
Circulation	Under review
Circulation	Access Services
Circulation/Reserves	Access Services
Circulation Department and another department called IRRC/ILL and another department within undergraduate library called Media/Reserves	We are currently considering changes to our access services that will probably result in some consolidations.

3. If the department is now called Access Services, in what year was that name first used and what was the department called previously? N=46

	Number of Departments called "Access Services"
<1981	3
1981–1985	4
1986–1990	6
1991–1995	10
1996–2000	15
2001–2005	8

"Access" Year	Previous Name
1976/77	Circulation
1978	Circulation Department
1980	Circulation and Stacks was one department. Reserve was its own department. ILL reported to reference
1982	Circulation
1985	Previously there was no collective term for the several units overseen by the Circulation Librarian: Circulation, General Reserve, Interlibrary Loan, Periodicals Center, Microforms, Annex Storage Facility, Photoduplication, and Undergraduate Library service units.
1985	Main Loan Desk
1985/86	Loan Department (included only Circulation, Stacks & Reserves)
1986	Merged Olin Circulation and Interlibrary Services; also took on Annex
1987	Circulation
1988	Separate departments for Circulation, Reserves, and Interlibrary Loan
1990	Central Circulation Services
1990	Each unit was individually identified (circ, reserve, ILL, etc.)
1990	Circulation/Access (Reserve, Stacks and ILL were in different divisions)
1991	Two separate departments (circulation and ILL)
1991	Circulation
1991	Circulation Services
1992	Circulation, separate from Periodical Information and ILL
1993	Circulation Services Department
1993	Separate units reporting elsewhere
1993/1994	Circulation Department
<1994	Circulation Services

1994	Circulation Department
1994	Circulation, Reserves, Interlibrary Loan
1996	Circulation Department
1996	Three departments: Circulation; Course Reserves/Current Periodicals; Interlibrary Loan
1996	Circulation
1996	Circulation Services (which included Reserve, Current Journals and Copy Services), Interlibrary Loan Department, Culpeper Media Library (separate departments)
1997	Access Services, Humanities and History Division
1997	Circulation, Interlibrary Loan and Facilities
1997	All separate, uncoordinated departments reporting to library director (Circulation, ILS, etc.)
1997	Circulation
1998	Circulation
1998	Circulation
1998	Circulation, Reserves, Current Periodicals, Microforms, Stacks/Storage
1999	Circulation Department
~2000	User Services
2000	Circulation Services
2000	Two departments: SML Circ, CCL Circ/Reserves
2001	It didn't exist as currently configured. Circulation Department encompassed reserves, circulation and stacks. When ILL was added in 2001 the name changed to Access Services.
2001	Circulation
2001	Circulation Services
2001	Stack Maintenance and Delivery
2003	Circulation
2003	Circulation
2004	General Services
2005	We expect to change from Circulation to Access Services in the next couple of months.

CHANGES IN DEPARTMENT ACTIVITIES

4. Please indicate whether the circulation/access services department or another department had responsibility for the following activities 10 years ago and which has responsibility for them today. Select N/A if the library did not or does not have responsibility for a particular activity. Also indicate which activities, if any, the circulation/access services department plans to add to its responsibilities in the near future (next one to five years). Check all that apply. N=73

Activity	1995			2005			Near Future	
	Circ / Access	Other Dept	N/A	Circ / Access	Other Dept	N/A	Will Add	Won't Add
Circulation	72	1	—	72	1	—	1	—
Stacks maintenance (reshelving, etc.)	64	9	—	64	9	—	—	6
Billing	64	4	4	61	6	3	—	5
Entry and/or exit control	57	15	—	55	17	—	1	7
Reserves	55	15	2	63	8	2	1	3
Study-room/carrel registration	50	15	6	47	16	8	1	8
Retrieval from offsite storage	41	8	24	48	9	14	5	5
Library security	41	27	4	41	29	2	1	13
Interlibrary loan	36	36	1	50	22	1	6	2
Current periodicals and/or newspapers	32	41	—	38	34	1	1	13
Microforms	25	47	1	32	37	4	—	19
On-campus document delivery	21	21	31	42	17	14	10	3
Photocopy services	21	39	13	17	36	18	5	23
Transporting materials to and from other libraries	19	47	7	21	45	6	1	18
Multimedia	17	46	10	29	37	7	2	17
Electronic reserves	16	8	47	59	9	4	2	3
Information desk services	16	48	9	22	42	9	2	18
Circulation of laptops	9	9	54	27	14	31	4	18
System administration for ILS	6	62	4	10	58	2	1	25
Bindery and/or labeling	5	66	2	7	63	3	2	31
Preservation	5	65	3	3	67	3	1	29
Other activity	14	7	2	20	3	—	—	—

Please Specify Other Activity

1995	2005	Description
Circ/Access	Circ/Access	Americans with Disabilities Act (ADA) services
Circ/Access	Circ/Access	Library staff IT support was available in both 1995 and 2005 through circ/access services; Library electronic classroom IT support was not available in 1995, available in 2005 through circ/access services.
Circ/Access	Circ/Access	Copy/print card sales
Circ/Access	Circ/Access	Manage contract of transport of material to and from [campus] libraries
Circ/Access	Circ/Access	Services for users with disabilities, lost and found, signage
Circ/Access	Circ/Access	Library Office for Persons with Disabilities is staffed by Access Services. It offers a suite of assistive technology for the benefit of students and other library users. Course materials are scanned and edited so that speech synthesizers such as JAWS can be applied to the texts.
Circ/Access	Circ/Access	Catalog maintenance/record updating
Circ/Access	Circ/Access	Copyright issues, alert (SDI) services
Circ/Access	Circ/Access	Computer lab general maintenance
Circ/Access	Circ/Access	Book Retrieval from Closed Stacks
Circ/Access	Circ/Access	Space Planning & Management
Circ/Access	Other Department	Lockers
Circ/Access	Other Department	Distance learning
Circ/Access; Other Department	Circ/Access	Friends of the Library memberships (evenings and weekends), NA in 1995, Access in 2005; Theatre bookings/film showings, Access in 1995 and 2005; Activation of copy/print cards, Other in 1995, Access in 2005; Lost and found, Access in 1995 and 2005
N/A	Circ/Access	Processing consortium loans
N/A	Circ/Access; Other Department	Information Commons will be a shared space between reference and circulation and will have some shared activities; also a new multimedia center on the main floor will open mid 2005 and assume laptop circulation duties, amongst other production & training with multi media; alumni services will be added to ILL services in 2005
Other Department	Circ/Access	Building Services/Shipping & Receiving
Other Department	Circ/Access	Copyright clearance
Other Department	Circ/Access	Music listening area
Other Department	Circ/Access	Shipping & Receiving and supplies

Other Department	Circ/Access	In-house printing services
Other Department	Circ/Access	Industrial & Business Information Service
Other Department	Circ/Access	Ready reference

5. Please indicate which of the following workflows were automated 10 years ago and which are automated today. Select N/A if the workflow is not applicable to your library. Also indicate if there are plans to automate any workflows in the near future (next one to five years). Check all that apply. N=73

Workflow	1995			2005			Near Future	
	Auto	Not	N/A	Auto	Not	N/A	Will Automate	Won't Automate
Entry and/or exit control (e.g., "swipe card" access, Checkpoint or 3M security system, etc.)	44	23	6	56	11	6	1	1
Notices (e.g., e-mail overdue notices, etc.)	34	38	1	71	2	—	2	—
Billing (e.g., e-mail bills, etc.)	28	41	4	63	5	5	3	2
Interlibrary loan (e.g., unmediated requesting, ILL management software, etc.)	26	43	4	67	5	1	1	1
Accounting (e.g., automatic transfers to bursar accounts, etc.)	22	38	10	38	24	8	9	—
Bindery and/or labeling (e.g., using ABLE software, printing labels from ILS module, etc.)	20	29	20	47	6	18	1	1
Stacks maintenance (e.g., electronic data capture, etc.)	7	57	7	13	50	8	9	10

Study-room/carrel registration	7	53	11	21	40	11	9	12
On-campus document delivery (e.g., electronic delivery, etc.)	6	48	18	47	12	11	7	1
Retrieval from offsite storage (e.g., robotic retrieval and delivery, electronic document delivery, etc.)	5	46	21	26	32	12	5	6
Multimedia reservations	4	41	28	20	28	23	6	3
Other workflow	2	3	3	8	—	—	—	—

Please Specify Other Workflow

1995	2005	Description
Automated	Automated	Holds/recalls
Automated	Automated	Patron loads
N/A	Automated	Laptop circulation; scanning for e-reserves; training augmented using instructional software (Blackboard)
N/A	Automated	Copyright clearance
N/A	Automated	Scanning/posting for e-reserves
Not automated	Automated	Searches/recalls
Not automated	Automated	Payroll deduction for university employees and collection agency submissions for non-affiliated users
Not automated	Automated	Patron holds; library-to-library requests; e-mail communication with patrons

6. Please indicate whether the circulation/access services department or another department offered the following self-service, patron-initiated, unmediated, and/or digital services to library users 10 years ago and which offers them today. Select N/A if the library did not or does not offer a particular service. Also indicate which services, if any, the circulation/access services department plans to add to its responsibilities in the near future (next one to five years). Check all that apply. N=73

Service	1995			2005			Near Future	
	Circ / Access	Other Dept	N/A	Circ / Access	Other Dept	N/A	Will Add	Won't Add
Online renewals	16	—	56	68	2	3	1	2
Online ILL requesting	13	9	50	50	20	3	3	1
Online offsite storage retrieval requesting	12	1	60	53	5	14	5	—
Self-check for circulation	9	—	64	30	2	39	13	13
Information kiosk	5	8	58	4	15	52	7	15
Electronic document delivery	4	7	60	49	15	8	7	2
Online study-room/carrel registration	4	1	66	15	8	47	12	12
Digital microform readers	1	3	67	20	31	18	9	8
Online multimedia reservations	1	5	66	12	19	39	9	12
Other service	3	—	5	8	—	—	—	—

Please Specify Other Service

1995	2005	Description
Circ/Access	Circ/Access	Patron-initiated, unmediated borrowing from consortia institutions
Circ/Access	Circ/Access	Recalls
Circ/Access	Circ/Access	Ability to place holds, recalls, and review personal accounts; self-check (implemented in 1996)
N/A	Circ/Access	Privileges renewal for alumni, spouses/partners of faculty, students, or staff
N/A	Circ/Access	Online recall/hold requests
N/A	Circ/Access	Faculty Authorization (Proxy Borrowing requests); reserve-list submissions
N/A	Circ/Access	Distance Learning Requesting
N/A	Circ/Access	Online, unmediated holds and library-to-library requests

7. Please indicate which of the following service points were administered by the circulation/access services department in 1995 and which the department administers today. Also indicate how many hours per week each service point was/is staffed. Check all that apply. N=73

Administered by Circ/Access		
	1995	2005
Circulation desk	72	72
Reserves desk	57	61
Stacks maintenance/ assistance	53	55
Entrance/exit desk	47	46
Billing desk	46	47
Interlibrary loan desk	43	50
Current periodicals	34	39
Microforms	28	38
Offsite storage	24	38
Media desk	20	27
Information desk	16	21
Laptop circulation	9	28
Other service point	12	14

Hours per Week Staffed in 1995						
	N	Min	Max	Mean	Median	Std Dev
Entrance/exit desk	41	82	120	100.7	102.0	9.5
Reserves desk	52	40	144	97.8	100.0	16.6
Circulation desk	63	37	144	96.7	100.0	17.0
Current periodicals	30	51	120	90.6	93.5	15.1
Media desk	16	40	108	85.8	93.3	21.5
Information desk	15	51	110	85.5	90.0	19.1
Microforms	26	50	108	83.8	87.0	17.7
Laptop circulation	6	40	101	78.5	90.0	26.6
Stacks maintenance/ assistance	44	40	144	76.9	84.3	26.9
Billing desk	38	35	112	63.6	45.8	28.3
Interlibrary loan desk	41	37	100	48.6	42.5	17.1
Offsite storage	19	8	95	42.6	40.0	24.6
Other service point	11	40	133	69.7	58.5	32.6

Hours per Week Staffed in 2005						
	N	Min	Max	Mean	Median	Std Dev
Entrance/exit desk	42	40	160	105.7	107.0	20.2
Reserves desk	56	40	160	105.6	104.0	22.7
Circulation desk	66	37	160	101.1	101.0	23.2
Laptop circulation	25	40	146	100.6	100.8	22.4
Current periodicals	32	40	154	95.9	100.4	25.5
Information desk	19	48	117	90.1	90.0	20.8
Media desk	22	40	154	88.8	86.3	30.9
Microforms	34	30	154	87.4	88.8	26.5
Stacks maintenance/ assistance	49	37	154	79.6	83.0	30.9
Billing desk	40	37	160	74.9	77.3	33.7
Interlibrary loan desk	45	37	114	53.6	95.0	22.7
Offsite storage	29	0	110	46.5	40.0	24.1
Other service point	13	35	133	75.3	60.0	35.2

Please Specify Other Service Point

1995	Hours	2005	Hours	Description
x	40.0	x	80.5	Math Collection circulation
x	40.0	x	40.0	Office for Services to People with Disabilities, staffed 40 hours/week, open 117.25 hours/week
x	42.5	x	42.5	Document delivery desk
x	42.5	x	42.5	Special Collections
x	50.0	x	50.0	Privileges desk
x	58.5	x	58.5	Book Service retrieval desks
x	60.0	x	60.0	ADA service area
x	96.0	x	114.0	Copy services/current journals
x	101.0	x	117.0	Undergraduate Library Services/Information Commons circulation desk
x	103.0	x	120.0	Study centers
x	133.0	x	133.0	Study room
		x	35.0	All night study space
		x	85.6	Digital Media Lab

If any of the services listed above were or are provided from the same desk/service point, please indicate the name of that service point and list the services provided. Describe up to **three** combined services desks. N=59

Service Point Name	1995 (N=42)	2005 (N=54)
Circulation	28	30
Reserves/Periodicals	6	4
Circulation/Reserves	5	13
Reserves	4	4
Audiovisual/Media Services	3	3
Current Periodicals/Microforms	2	2
Access Services	1	5
Service Desk	1	5
Miscellaneous other names	5	15

Services Provided	1995	2005
Circulation	Circulation, reserves, ILL, billing, entrance/exit security, stack maintenance and assistance, consortial borrowing, remote storage retrieval, information, laptops, external user cards, photocopy delivery, computer lab	Same plus video retrieval, study room reservations, ADA services, journal circulation, Internet access for external users
Reserves/Periodicals	Reserves, current periodical assistance, microforms, periodical circulation, newspaper maintenance, group study room assignments	Same plus laptops
Circulation/Reserves	Circulation, reserves, billing, entrance/exit security, remote storage retrieval, laptops, current periodicals	Same plus ILL pickup, stacks assistance, media bookings, microform assistance
Reserves	Reserves, media, newspapers, microforms, ADA services, circulation	Same plus electronic reserves, laptops
Audiovisual/Media Services	Media, microforms, periodicals, reserves	Same plus headset and other equipment rental
Current Periodicals/ Microforms	Periodicals, newspapers, microforms	Same plus videos and viewing stations
Access Services	Circulation, reserves, ILL, billing, entrance/exit security, stacks	Same plus document delivery, e-reserves, laptops, photocopy, network printing
Service Desk	Circulation, reserves, billing, entrance/exit security	Same plus information, ILL, laptops, stacks, current periodicals, microforms

8. What is the title of the head of the circulation/access services department? N=73

Head,/Head of Access Services	23	32%
Head,/Head of Circulation Services/Department	7	10%
Director,/Director of Access Services	4	5%
Head,/Head of Access & Delivery Services	4	5%
Coordinator,/Coordinator of/for Access Services	3	4%
Access Services Librarian	2	3%
Head, Circulation & Interlibrary Services/Loan	2	3%
Other title	28	38%

Please Specify Other Title

Access Services Department Chair

Assistant Director for Access & Facilities

Associate Dean, Access & Delivery

Chair, Access Services

Chief of Access and Reader Services

Chief, Collections Access, Loan and Management Division

Circulation and Media Services

Circulation Librarian

Circulation Services Director

Circulation Services Manager

Circulation Supervisor

Department Chair, Access & Branch Services

Director of Information Access and Delivery Services

Director of Library Access Services

Director, Access Services, Arts & Sciences Libraries

Director, Collection Services

Division Leader, Access Services

Head of Customer Services

Head of Onsite Access Services

Head, Access Services & Government Publications/Maps/Law Library

Head, Access Services/Interlibrary Loan

Head, Borrower Services

Head, Customer and Access Services Department

Head, Resource Support Services

Public Services Librarian

Service Point Coordinator

Team Leader

No Head—Management Team consisting of four managers

9. **To whom does this person report? N=73**

Library dean/director	15	21%
Assistant/associate dean/director for public services	36	49%
Assistant/associate dean/director for technical services	3	4%
Assistant/associate dean/director for collection development	—	—
Other position	19	26%

Please Specify Other Position Title

Assistant Vice President of University Libraries

Associate Dean for University Park Libraries

Associate Dean of Administrative Services

Associate Dean, Access, Bibliographic and Information Services

Associate University Librarian for Access Services

Associate University Librarian for Access Services & Systems

Associate University Librarian for Collections and Access

Associate University Librarian for Research Services & Collections

Deputy Director

Director General, Care of Collections Branch

Director of Administrative Services

Director of Humanities and Social Sciences Services

Director of Information Services

Director, Collections and Services Directorate

Director, Organizational Services

Head, Access and Digital Services Division

Head, Holland/New Library

Head, Public Services

Head, Social Sciences & Humanities Library

10. Has the number of circulation/access services department positions for each staff category below increased, decreased, or stayed about the same since 1995? Please indicate the current number of FTE for each staff category. N=72

	Increased	Decreased	Same	Total Number of Responses
Student assistant	27	23	20	70
Support staff	21	37	11	69
Librarian	22	19	27	68
Other professional	16	6	27	49
Other staff category	6	2	—	8
Total Number of Responses	49	53	50	

Please Specify Other Staff Category that Increased

Managers

Non-student assistants

Security guard

Service/Maintenance

Supervisory Staff

Wage payroll employees

Please Specify Other Staff Category that Decreased

Part-time assistants

Special Project contracts

2005 FTE	N	Min	Max	Mean	Median	Std Dev
Librarian	63	0	9	1.8	1.0	1.8
Support staff	63	0	135	23.1	21.0	17.9
Student assistant	55	0	75	23.6	18.0	18.3
Other professional	43	0	14	2.5	2.0	3.1
Other staff category	8	0	23	6.9	3.8	7.5

2005 Librarian FTE (N=60)	Increased	Decreased	Same
0	—	5	6
1	2	8	12
2	4	1	5
3	8	1	2
4	2	—	—
5	1	—	—
6	—	1	—
7	—	—	—
8	—	1	—
9	1	—	—

2005 Support Staff FTE (N=59)	Increased	Decreased	Same
0–9	2	5	—
10–19	5	11	4
20–29	6	11	3
30–39	3	4	—
40–49	2	1	1
50+	1	—	—

2005 Student Assistant FTE (N=54)	Increased	Decreased	Same
0–9	4	4	1
10–19	7	9	4
20–29	8	2	4
30–39	—	1	1
40–49	1	—	1
50+	3	1	3

2005 Other professional FTE (N=40)	Increased	Decreased	Same
0	—	—	12
1	2	1	4
2	3	—	3
3	2	1	1
4	1	1	1
5	3	—	—
6	—	1	—
7+	4	—	—

11. Have circulation/access services staff been cross-trained among various tasks and/or units or have they specialized in one particular activity? N=73

	1995	2005	Total Number of Responses
Cross-trained	25	59	61
Specialized	55	29	58
Total Number of Responses	70	72	

Selected Comments from Respondents

"Staff cross-trained within stacks, circulation, reserve. Some interlibrary loan work also handled by stacks or circulation/reserve staff. Some cross-training with reference for service to online databases, in particular by evening staff and staff in periodicals/videos/microforms who handle a lot of information queries related to databases."

"All staff members are trained to assist at the circulation desk."

"70% are specialized; 30% are cross-trained."

"Limited amount of cross training for some functions between circulation and stacks students and staff, and between circulation & ILL staff for ILL circulation outside ILL office hours."

"Combined desks have led to cross-training."

"There is some specialization, e.g., electronic reserve. Other functions, especially the service point, are all cross-trained."

"There has been some cross-training between reserve and circulation. Media staff have been trained in circulation desk functions."

"Reserves and circulation cross-trained; storage and document delivery cross-trained."

"Cross-training not required or expected, but some staff routinely perform the duties of other staff."

"Although staff in particular units are specialized, they are cross-trained so they can assist in other Circulation units either routinely or on an as-needed basis."

"ILL staff are cross-trained in all aspects of ILL. Just about everyone knows the basics of all types of circulation. Further cross-training will come as we physically merge the separate units in the very near future."

"ILL borrowing and lending staff are cross trained to handle each other's work. Some ILL staff are cross-trained in current periodicals. Some current periodicals staff are cross-trained in reserve. All reserve staff are cross-trained in circulation. Some circulation staff are partly cross-trained in reserve. Three ILL staff are cross-trained with circulation. One reserve staff is cross-trained with ILL. One ILL staff is cross trained with a branch circulation."

"Microform and media center staff are cross-trained; satellite (offsite) staff are cross-trained in circulation; overnight staff are cross-trained in circulation and reserves; some circulation staff are cross-trained in bookstacks."

"As we add ILL and copy services, the cross training will increase. Since 1994 Access Services has been doing some duties for ILL: retrieving/processing our books for other libraries, photocopying journal articles, checking out ILL materials. We currently do that plus scan articles."

"Circulation services staff provide basic ILL customer service support since the office space merged. ILL and circulation services staff provide back-up for the onsite storage facility."

"In the very near future we will be cross-training circulation and stacks students. Stacks currently do all searching and retrieval for circulation."

"Cross training is fairly new; only within past year or two is it really taking hold."

"Changes in staffing levels necessitated cross-training in 1999; changes in service delivery required further cross-training in 2003."

There has been limited cross-training between circulation and other inventory management tasks such as quality control, inventorying the collections, and searching for items not readily located when requested."

"Cross-training, is mostly due to cuts in salary and budgets; need to streamline."

12. Does the circulation/access services department have a distinct operating budget? N=74

Yes	37	50%
No	37	50%

If yes, what is the operating budget for the 2005 fiscal year? N=33

Min	Max	Mean	Median
$66,000	$4,000,000	$686,220	$300,000

Budget	N
$66,000–99,999	3
$100,000–199,999	7
$200,000–299,999	6
$300,000–399,999	5
$400,000-499,999	1
$500,000–999,999	5
$1,000,000–1,999,999	1
$2,000,000–2,999,999	4
$4,000,000	1

13. What cost and/or expenditure categories does this budget cover? Check all that apply. N=37

Student wages	36	97%
Office supplies	23	62%
Reprographics and printing	19	51%
Full- and part-time personnel	18	49%
Office equipment	18	49%
Repair of office equipment	17	46%
Telecommunications	14	38%
Postage	13	35%
Rental of office equipment	11	30%
Other category	10	27%

Please Specify Other Category

Office equipment under $500.00

Equipment less than $500

Travel support

Facilities repairs, collections moves

Travel, discretionary funds, some general office supplies, some specialized budgets

ILL borrowing has a budget for paying for items borrowed and copyright compliance that is in the Acquisitions budget.

Full-time wage positions but not full-time salaried staff positions

Special Project contracts

Staff training

Contracts, minor budget items, standing offers

14. **What level of budgetary responsibility resides with the department head? Check all that apply. N=62**

Manages student wages budget	55	89%
Manages supplies budget	25	40%
Manages equipment budget	15	24%
Manages personnel budget	14	23%
Other	17	27%

Please Specify Other Category

Interlibrary loan income budget

Equipment less than $500

Travel

Accounts related to ILL activities and copyright clearance

Revolving fund of revenues from special services for businesses, etc.

Special Project contracts

Staff Training

Makes equipment purchase suggestions.

Budget is centrally managed—department head has input at the budget planning level.

Prepares annual equipment allocation request and purchases equipment.

Department head oversees cost center managers who manage their own budgets in the categories listed above.

Department head orders equipment and supplies, but doesn't have separate budget. We are told what student budget is.

Monitor the student budget and the equipment budget; most of the budget work is done in administration.

SERVICE EVALUATION

15. **What techniques does the library use to evaluate the effectiveness of the circulation/access services department's services? Check all that apply. N=73**

Track the number of circulation transactions	72	99%
Track usage of Web pages, ILS, e-reserves, etc.	56	77%
LibQUAL+™ survey	51	70%
Track qualitative data on interlibrary loan transactions	44	60%
Conduct user surveys	40	55%
Interview external users (e.g., researchers, faculty, students) of the services	34	47%
Conduct focus groups	28	38%
Interview internal users (e.g., library staff) of the services	26	36%
Other technique	16	22%

Please Specify Other Technique

Exit count

Solicit comments

Workflow analysis from outside consultants

Online and paper comment cards

ARL & RLG document delivery analysis

Annual review of staff

Entrance/exit statistics, head counts during 24/7

Faculty board; student board

Online suggestion boxes

Library-designed surveys, usability studies

Web comments

ADDITIONAL COMMENTS

16. Please submit any additional information regarding the circulation/access services department's activities and responsibilities that may assist us in accurately analyzing the results of this survey.

Selected Comments from Respondents

"Our library budget is flexible, allowing us to allocate department budgets and work within the allocation, and supplement a department budget when needed. Staff, student staff wages are included, as well as exceptional equipment purchases, supplies, maintenance contracts (current and new) and promotional materials used in orientation or special events. As manager, I recommend the student wage amount, equipment purchases, and personnel promotions.

We sometimes use quantitative automated data to reflect BI sessions' results (increased department ILL, for instance, or increased grad activity in consortia borrowing or ILL, patron type data from entrance data during 24x7 after-business hours.) Focus groups and feedback events are now used to evaluate library services, space, changes as we move to an Information Commons model for our main floor; user surveys are included in this redesign."

"The Loan/Reserve Desk is 100% managed by students from hour-to-hour: we have 7–8 student managers during fall/spring semesters who supervise all of the other students in hourly shifts. These managers report to permanent staff supervisors in the department."

"Electronic Reserves was a pilot project in 1995. Information desk services are still in transition from reference area to circulation main desk function. Study-room registration does not exist, only carrels. Carrel registration is only available 3 times/year. Access services has a billing coordinator who communicates with the university bursar's office. There is no separate billing desk here, but questions about library fines can be asked at the main circulation desk at any time, in person or by phone. There is an information kiosk team at the present time and they are determining the best way to develop an information kiosk. Patrons can receive assistance regarding microforms in the Culpeper Media Library. In terms of student staffing, DD/ILL's student staffing has increased, but circulation/reserve's staffing has significantly decreased, probably by 50%. In addition, please note that the area budget handles student labor funding for student employees. We have many work-study students and they are not paid out of any library funds."

"We are currently in the process of streamlining our organization so that we can make better use of our staff while still providing timely expert service where needed."

"1995 was the year Access Services was formed for the first time. In 1999, the head of that department left and Access Services was dispersed to Reference and Collection Management. Just about a week ago (!), Access Services was reconstituted, with a few changes. Periodical Information, which reported to Access

Services, remains with Reference. Billing now reports to the fiscal officer. Copyright Clearance, a department formed in 1999 reporting to Media Services, now reports to Access Services."

"ADS Department also offers and manages a petition and appeal process by which borrowers can contest charges for lost/overdue items, etc. This includes an appeals committee of faculty and students."

"The libraries' Office for Persons with Disabilities is included in the administration of Access Services. This office collaborates with the university's Office for Disability Services which refers students to the libraries' office according to their criteria. The libraries also provide service to walk-in users when needed. Staffed with 1 full time and .5 FTE, the office is equipped with a full suite of assistive technology to provide services for the visually impaired, physically impaired, hearing impaired, and learning impaired. Demand on this service is increasing exponentially.
Responsibility for the exit control/information desks will be assumed by Public Services in the next fiscal year in an effort to provide more extensive services.
The Access Services Council, made up of librarians and paralibrarians representing 36 libraries across 24 campuses, has responsibility for coordinating services, recommending policy, and management initiatives. The council is appointed by the Head of Access Services."

"The Arts & Sciences Libraries, encompassing the Architecture & Planning Library, Lockwood Memorial Library, Sciences & Engineering Library, and the Undergraduate Library, were administratively restructured in 2001 and are now overseen by an administrative team of four directors with responsibilities in specific functional areas: access services, collections & research services, public services, and university & external relations. The four directors report to the Assistant Vice President of University Libraries."

"The library has recently conducted an organizational review and restructured Access Services to Access and Preservation Services. The new department will be headed by a librarian and include circulation, reserves, stacks management, interlibrary loan, and preservation. The new department will report to Collection Services. Changes will take effect no later than May 1, 2005."

"In September 1999, the support staff became unionized, the Circulation Department and the Processing Department merged and was named Access Services. We began to use student assistants for the bulk of hours dedicated to stacks maintenance. This increased the number of staff employed at that time. With the move to electronic resources, the print collection activity declined markedly and it follows naturally that the number of student assistants employed has since decreased.
In September 2003, the Reference Desk and the Circulation Desk were demolished and a new single desk for all services was constructed. The services that were provided at the two desks are now handled at this one desk but with referral for in-depth reference. The Access Services unit was renamed Resource Support Services. All staff, both professional and paraprofessional, have front line service duties in their job descriptions as well as their own specific areas of responsibility. The FTE information in question #10 reflects Resource Support staff allotted for front line service and not the time allotted for reserves processing, materials handling, interlibrary loans. These FTE hours alone are not sufficient to staff the service desk. The remaining coverage is provided by the Research & Instructional Services staff."

"Because the library no longer has a single department overseeing traditional 'access service' activities, I answered 'NO' to question #1. However, you may be interested in the following information. In 1995, the library did have a department known as Access Services, which at the time consisted of Circulation, Stacks Management, Interlibrary Loan & Document Delivery, Reserve, Periodical Reading Room, Media, Microforms,

Map Room, and Photoduplication. In 2003, as part of a major library reorganization, the Access Services Department was discontinued. Most of the units in the former Access Services Department continue to exist within a newly formed Research and Access Division, but are organized as follows:

Circulation became part of a newly merged Circulation and Branch Facilities Department. The department head reports to the Associate Dean for Research & Access (AD/RA).

Stacks Management, Microforms, Periodical Reading Room, and Map Room all became part of a newly created Stacks and Service Desks Department. The department head reports to the AD/RA.

Reserve, Media, and ILL/Document Delivery became part of a newly created Digital Services Department. The department head reports to the AD/RA.

Photoduplication Services were outsourced to University Printing.

These three new departments, along with the departments of Special Collections and Preservation, comprise the new Research & Access Division."

RESPONDING INSTITUTIONS

University at Albany, SUNY
University of Alberta
Arizona State University
Auburn University
Boston College
Boston University
Brigham Young University
University of British Columbia
University at Buffalo, SUNY
University of California, Davis
University of California, Irvine
University of California, Riverside
University of California, San Diego
University of California, Santa Barbara
Case Western Reserve University
University of Chicago
Colorado State University
Columbia University
University of Connecticut
Cornell University
Dartmouth College
Duke University
Emory University
University of Florida
Florida State University
George Washington University
University of Guelph
University of Hawaii at Manoa
University of Houston
University of Illinois at Chicago
University of Illinois at Urbana-Champaign
Indiana University Bloomington
University of Iowa
Iowa State University
Johns Hopkins University
Kent State University
University of Kentucky
Library and Archives Canada
Library of Congress

University of Louisville
McMaster University
University of Miami
University of Michigan
Michigan State University
University of Minnesota
University of Missouri
University of Nebraska–Lincoln
New York Public Library
New York University
University of North Carolina at Chapel Hill
North Carolina State University
Northwestern University
University of Oklahoma
University of Oregon
University of Pennsylvania
Pennsylvania State University
University of Pittsburgh
Princeton University
Purdue University
University of Southern California
Southern Illinois University Carbondale
Syracuse University
Temple University
University of Tennessee
Texas A&M University
Tulane University
University of Utah
Vanderbilt University
University of Virginia
Virginia Tech
University of Washington
Washington State University
Washington University in St. Louis
University of Waterloo
University of Western Ontario
University of Wisconsin–Madison
Yale University

REPRESENTATIVE DOCUMENTS

Organization Charts

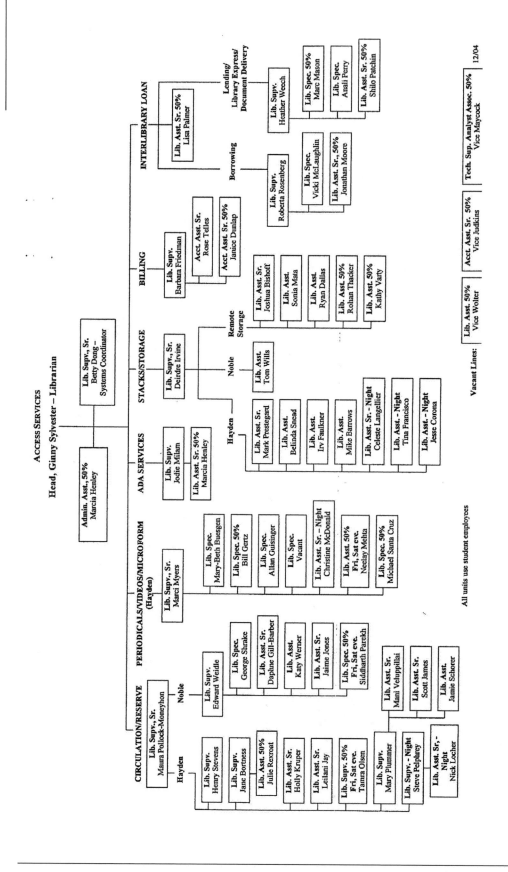

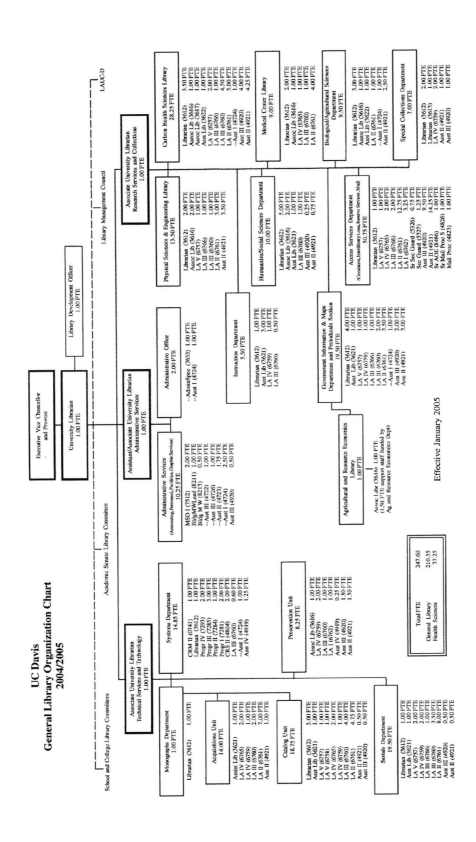

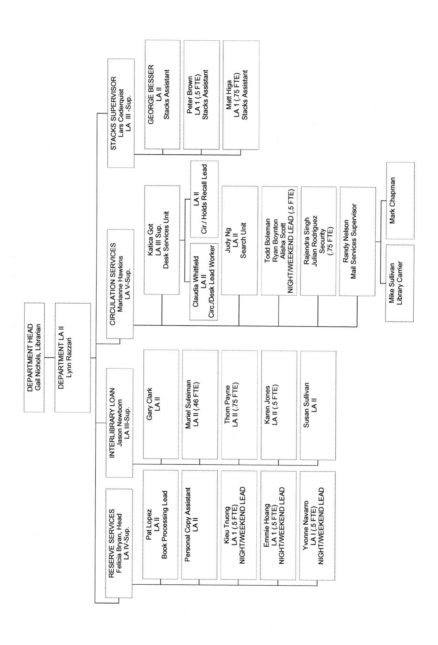

UCIrvine|LIBRARIES

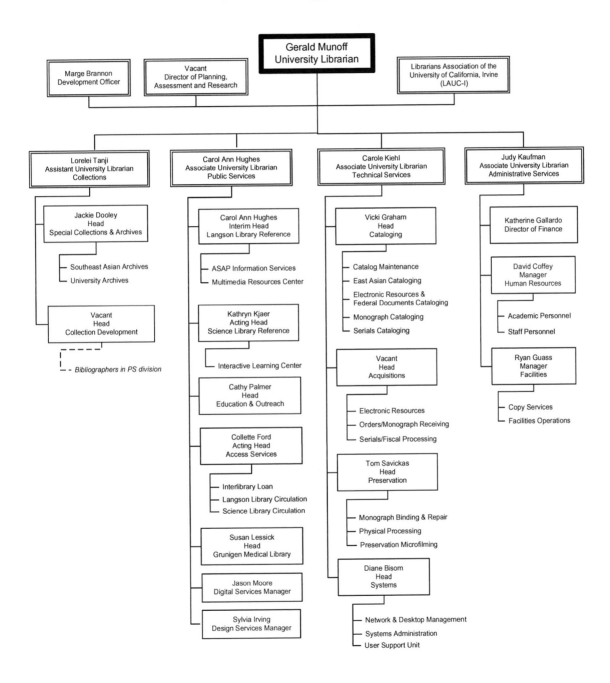

Gerald Munoff
University Librarian

Marge Brannon
Development Officer

Vacant
Director of Planning,
Assessment and Research

Librarians Association of the
University of California, Irvine
(LAUC-I)

Lorelei Tanji
Assistant University Librarian
Collections

Jackie Dooley
Head
Special Collections & Archives

— Southeast Asian Archives
— University Archives

Vacant
Head
Collection Development

- - Bibliographers in PS division

Carol Ann Hughes
Associate University Librarian
Public Services

Carol Ann Hughes
Interim Head
Langson Library Reference

— ASAP Information Services
— Multimedia Resources Center

Kathryn Kjaer
Acting Head
Science Library Reference

— Interactive Learning Center

Cathy Palmer
Head
Education & Outreach

Collette Ford
Acting Head
Access Services

— Interlibrary Loan
— Langson Library Circulation
— Science Library Circulation

Susan Lessick
Head
Grunigen Medical Library

Jason Moore
Digital Services Manager

Sylvia Irving
Design Services Manager

Carole Kiehl
Associate University Librarian
Technical Services

Vicki Graham
Head
Cataloging

— Catalog Maintenance
— East Asian Cataloging
— Electronic Resources &
Federal Documents Cataloging
— Monograph Cataloging
— Serials Cataloging

Vacant
Head
Acquisitions

— Electronic Resources
— Orders/Monograph Receiving
— Serials/Fiscal Processing

Tom Savickas
Head
Preservation

— Monograph Binding & Repair
— Physical Processing
— Preservation Microfilming

Diane Bisom
Head
Systems

— Network & Desktop Management
— Systems Administration
— User Support Unit

Judy Kaufman
Associate University Librarian
Administrative Services

Katherine Gallardo
Director of Finance

David Coffey
Manager
Human Resources

— Academic Personnel
— Staff Personnel

Ryan Guass
Manager
Facilities

— Copy Services
— Facilities Operations

October 1, 2005

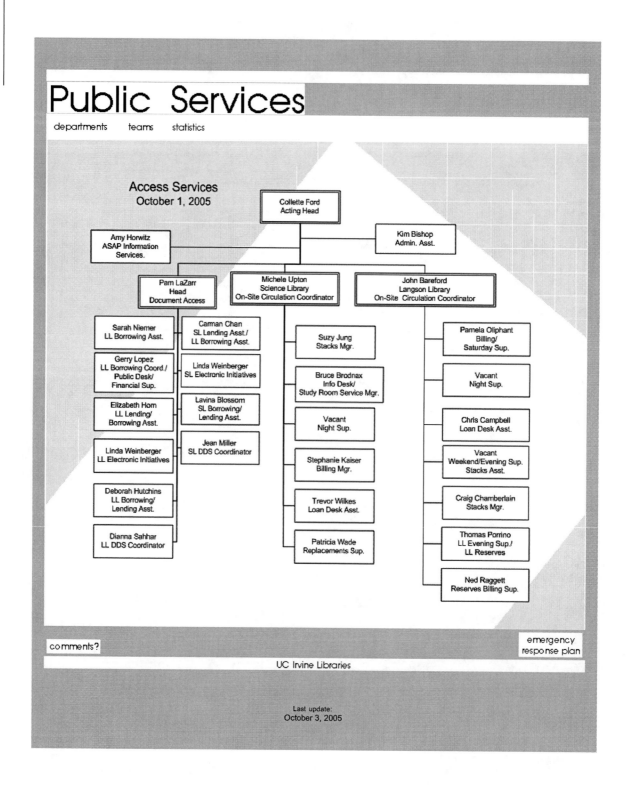

Davidson Library Organization Chart

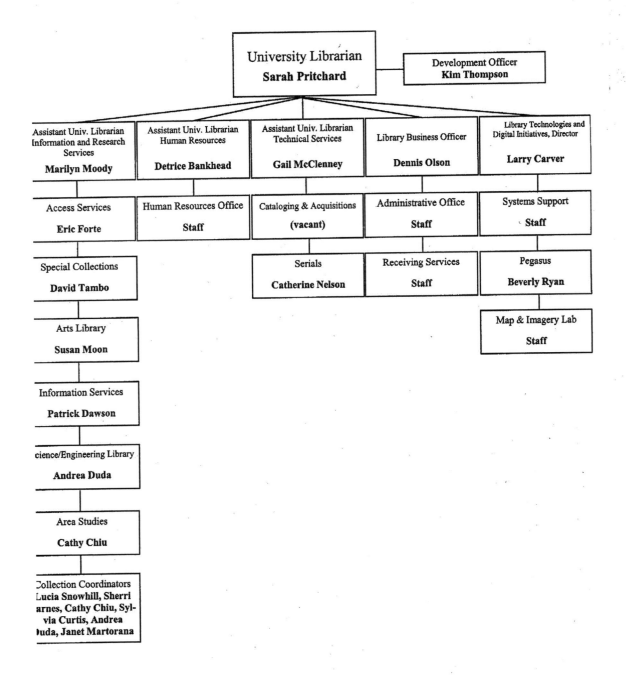

University Librarian
Sarah Pritchard

Development Officer
Kim Thompson

Assistant Univ. Librarian
Information and Research
Services
Marilyn Moody

Assistant Univ. Librarian
Human Resources
Detrice Bankhead

Assistant Univ. Librarian
Technical Services
Gail McClenney

Library Business Officer
Dennis Olson

Library Technologies and
Digital Initiatives, Director
Larry Carver

Access Services
Eric Forte

Human Resources Office
Staff

Cataloging & Acquisitions
(vacant)

Administrative Office
Staff

Systems Support
Staff

Special Collections
David Tambo

Serials
Catherine Nelson

Receiving Services
Staff

Pegasus
Beverly Ryan

Arts Library
Susan Moon

Map & Imagery Lab
Staff

Information Services
Patrick Dawson

Science/Engineering Library
Andrea Duda

Area Studies
Cathy Chiu

Collection Coordinators
**Lucia Snowhill, Sherri
Barnes, Cathy Chiu, Sylvia Curtis, Andrea
Duda, Janet Martorana**

ACCESS SERVICES

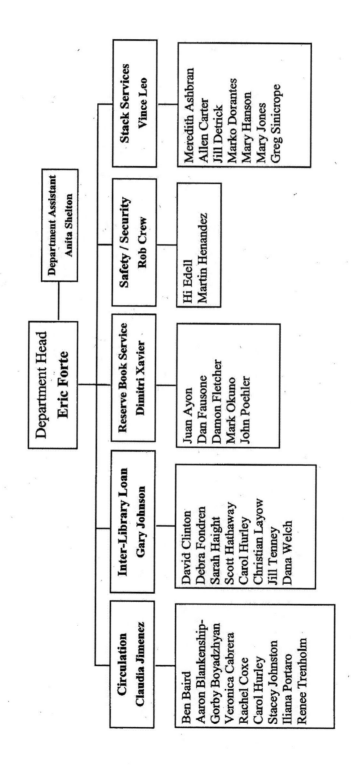

01/05/05

Department Head
Eric Forte

Department Assistant
Anita Shelton

Circulation
Claudia Jimenez

Ben Baird
Aaron Blankenship-
Gorby Boyadzhyan
Veronica Cabrera
Rachel Coxe
Carol Hurley
Stacey Johnston
Iliana Portaro
Renee Trenholm

Inter-Library Loan
Gary Johnson

David Clinton
Debra Fondren
Sarah Haight
Scott Hathaway
Carol Hurley
Christian Layow
Jill Tenney
Dana Welch

Reserve Book Service
Dimitri Xavier

Juan Ayon
Dan Fausone
Damon Fletcher
Mark Okuno
John Poehler

Safety / Security
Rob Crew

Hi Edell
Martin Henandez

Stack Services
Vince Leo

Meredith Ashbran
Allen Carter
Jill Detrick
Marko Dorantes
Mary Hanson
Mary Jones
Greg Sinicrope

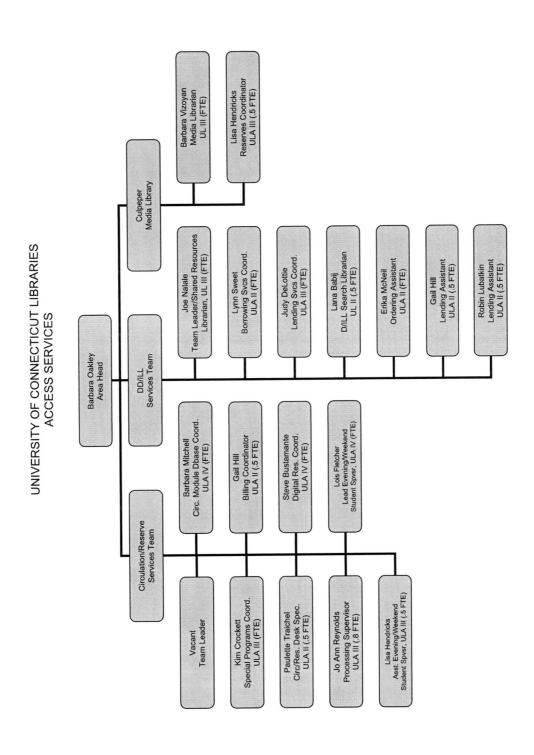

UNIVERSITY OF CONNECTICUT LIBRARIES
ACCESS SERVICES

Barbara Oakley
Area Head

Culpeper
Media Library

Barbara Vizoyan
Media Librarian
UL III (FTE)

Lisa Hendricks
Reserves Coordinator
ULA III (.5 FTE)

DD/ILL
Services Team

Joe Natale
Team Leader/Shared Resources
Librarian, UL III (FTE)

Lynn Sweet
Borrowing Svcs Coord.
ULA II (FTE)

Judy DeLottie
Lending Svcs Coord.
ULA III (FTE)

Lana Babij
D/ILL Search Librarian
UL II (.5 FTE)

Erika McNeil
Ordering Assistant
ULA II (FTE)

Gail Hill
Lending Assistant
ULA II (.5 FTE)

Robin Lubatkin
Lending Assistant
ULA II (.5 FTE)

Circulation/Reserve
Services Team

Barbara Mitchell
Circ. Module Dbase Coord.
ULA IV (FTE)

Gail Hill
Billing Coordinator
ULA II (.5 FTE)

Steve Bustamante
Digital Res. Coord.
ULA IV (FTE)

Lois Fletcher
Lead Evening/Weekend
Student Spvsr, ULA IV (FTE)

Vacant
Team Leader

Kim Crockett
Special Programs Coord.
ULA III (FTE)

Paulette Traichel
Circ/Res. Desk Spec.
ULA II (.5 FTE)

Jo Ann Reynolds
Processing Supervisor
ULA III (.8 FTE)

Lisa Hendricks
Asst. Evening/Weekend
Student Spvsr, ULA III (.5 FTE)

University *of* Florida   Hours | Ask a Librarian | Online Requests | Remote Logon

George A. Smathers Libraries   Library Catalog | Databases | Site Map | Help | Search

Library >> Staff Site >> Organization Chart

Organization Chart

```
Director of Libraries
Dale B. Canelas ---------|---  Public Services Division
                         |     Carol Turner, Associate Director
                         |
                         |---  Collection Management Division
                         |     John Ingram, Deputy Director
                         |
                         |---  Technology Services Division
                         |     Martha Hruska, Associate Director
                         |
                         |---  Support Services Division
                         |     Bill Covey, Interim Assistant Director
                         |
                         |---  Library Development
                         |     Sandra Fox Melching, Director of Development
                         |        |
                         |        |--- Public Information Officer
                         |--------------Barbara Hood
Public Services Division
Carol Turner ------------->|---  Humanities and Social Science Services
Associate Director         |        Gary Cornwell, Chair
                           |        |
                           |        |-- HSS Reference
                           |        |      (Colleen Seale, Asst. Chair)
                           |        |-- Architecture/Fine Arts Library
                           |        |      (Ann Lindell, Head)
                           |        |-- Education Library
                           |        |      (Iona Malanchuk, Head)
                           |        |-- Journalism Library
                           |        |      (Patrick Reakes, Head)
                           |---------- Music Library
                           |               (Robena Cornwell, Head)
                           |
                           |---  Access Services Department
                           |        Lori Driscoll, Chair
                           |        |
                           |        |--Library West Circulation and Retrieval Services
                           |        |--Electronic Reserve and Copyright Clearance
                           |        |--Storage and Collection Planning Services
                           |        |      (Benjamin Walker, Assistant Chair)
                           |        |--Interlibrary Loan Office
                           |               (Michelle Foss, Head)
                           |
                           |---  Government Documents Department
                           |        Jan Swanbeck, Chair
                           |        |
                           |        |--Map & Imagery Library
                           |               (HelenJane Armstrong, Head)
                           |
                           |---  Marston Science Library
                                    Carol Drum, Chair
```

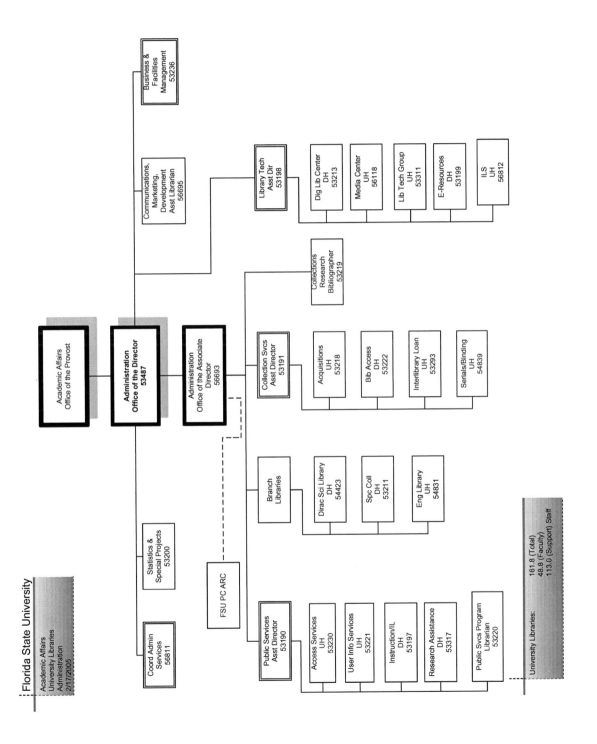

Florida State University

Academic Affairs
University Libraries
Administration
2/17/2005

Academic Affairs
Office of the Provost

Administration
Office of the Director
53487

Administration
Office of the Associate Director
56693

Business & Facilities Management
53236

Communications, Marketing, Development
Asst Librarian
56695

Statistics & Special Projects
53200

Coord Admin Services
56811

FSU PC ARC

Library Tech Asst Dir
53198

Dig Lib Center
DH
53213

Media Center
UH
56118

Lib Tech Group
UH
53311

E-Resources
DH
53199

ILS
UH
56812

Collections Research Bibliographer
53219

Collection Svcs Asst Director
53191

Acquisitions
UH
53218

Bib Access
DH
53222

Interlibrary Loan
UH
53293

Serials/Binding
UH
54839

Branch Libraries

Dirac Sci Library
DH
54423

Spc Coll
DH
53211

Eng Library
UH
54831

Public Services Asst Director
53190

Access Services
UH
53230

User Info Services
UH
53221

Instruction/IL
DH
53197

Research Assistance
DH
53317

Public Svcs Program Librarian
53220

University Libraries: 161.8 (Total)
48.8 (Faculty)
113.0 (Support) Staff

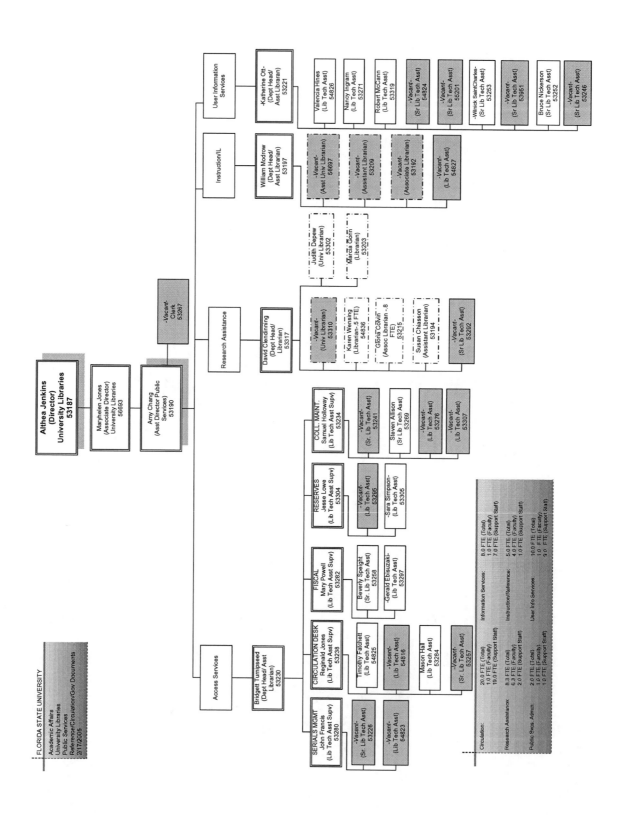

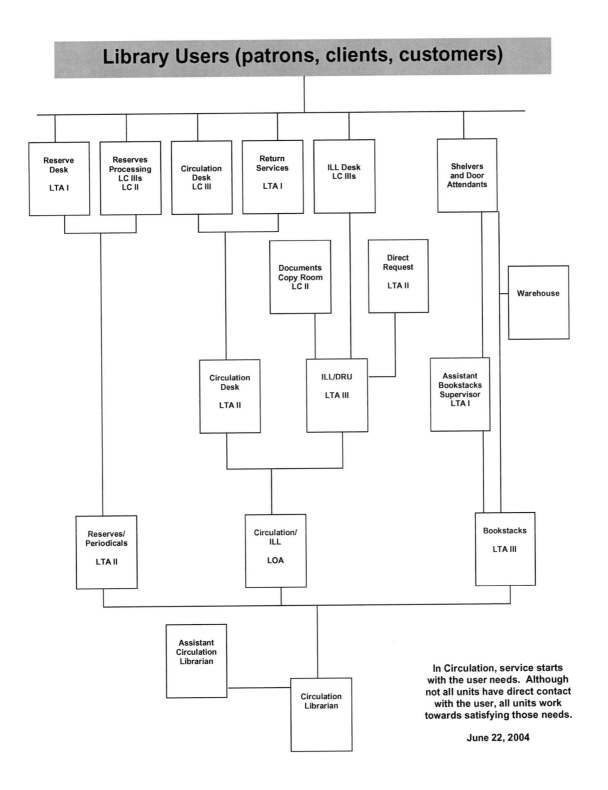

Library Users (patrons, clients, customers)

Reserve Desk
LTA I

Reserves Processing
LC IIIs
LC II

Circulation Desk
LC III

Return Services
LTA I

ILL Desk
LC IIIs

Shelvers and Door Attendants

Documents Copy Room
LC II

Direct Request
LTA II

Warehouse

Circulation Desk
LTA II

ILL/DRU
LTA III

Assistant Bookstacks Supervisor
LTA I

Reserves/Periodicals
LTA II

Circulation/ILL
LOA

Bookstacks
LTA III

Assistant Circulation Librarian

Circulation Librarian

In Circulation, service starts with the user needs. Although not all units have direct contact with the user, all units work towards satisfying those needs.

June 22, 2004

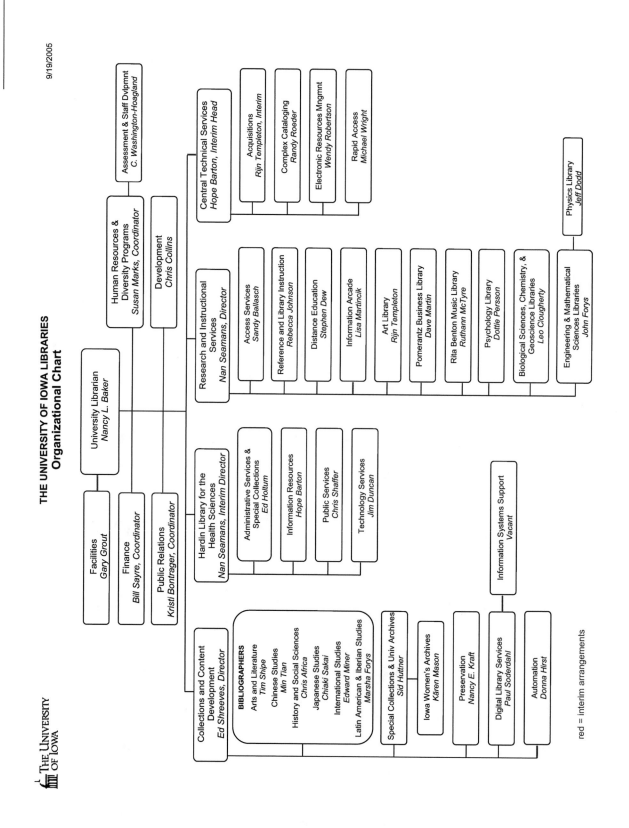

THE UNIVERSITY OF IOWA LIBRARIES
Organizational Chart

9/19/2005

University Librarian
Nancy L. Baker

Facilities
Gary Grout

Finance
Bill Sayre, Coordinator

Public Relations
Kristi Bontrager, Coordinator

Human Resources &
Diversity Programs
Susan Marks, Coordinator

Assessment & Staff Dvlpmnt
C. Washington-Hoagland

Development
Chris Collins

Central Technical Services
Hope Barton, Interim Head

Acquisitions
Rijn Templeton, Interim

Complex Cataloging
Randy Roeder

Electronic Resources Mngmnt
Wendy Robertson

Rapid Access
Michael Wright

Research and Instructional
Services
Nan Seamans, Director

Access Services
Sandy Ballasch

Reference and Library Instruction
Rebecca Johnson

Distance Education
Stephen Dew

Information Arcade
Lisa Martincik

Art Library
Rijn Templeton

Pomerantz Business Library
Dave Martin

Rita Benton Music Library
Ruthann McTyre

Psychology Library
Dottie Persson

Biological Sciences, Chemistry, &
Geoscience Libraries
Leo Clougherty

Engineering & Mathematical
Sciences Libraries
John Forys

Physics Library
Jeff Dodd

Hardin Library for the
Health Sciences
Nan Seamans, Interim Director

Administrative Services &
Special Collections
Ed Holtum

Information Resources
Hope Barton

Public Services
Chris Shaffer

Technology Services
Jim Duncan

Collections and Content
Development
Ed Shreeves, Director

BIBLIOGRAPHERS
Arts and Literature
Tim Shipe
Chinese Studies
Min Tian
History and Social Sciences
Chris Africa
Japanese Studies
Chiaki Sakai
International Studies
Edward Miner
Latin American & Iberian Studies
Marsha Forys

Special Collections & Univ Archives
Sid Huttner

Iowa Women's Archives
Kären Mason

Preservation
Nancy E. Kraft

Information Systems Support
Vacant

Digital Library Services
Paul Soderdahl

Automation
Donna Hirst

red = interim arrangements

THE UNIVERSITY
OF IOWA

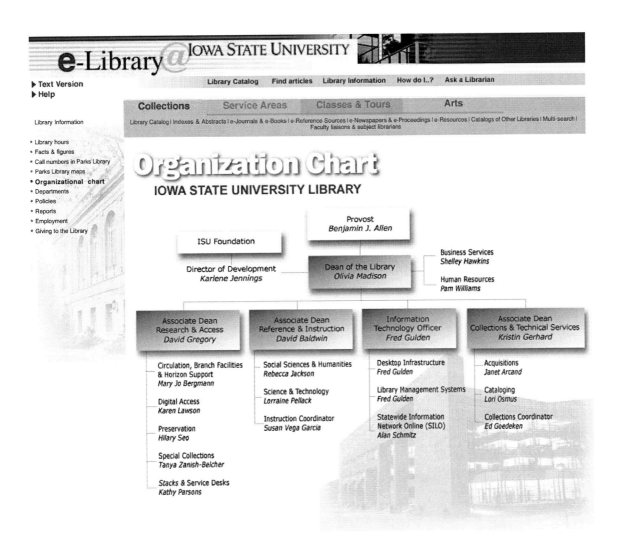

▶ Text Version
▶ Help

Library Information

* Library hours
* Facts & figures
* Call numbers in Parks Library
* Parks Library maps
* **Organizational chart**
* Departments
* Policies
* Reports
* Employment
* Giving to the Library

Library Catalog   Find articles   Library Information   How do I..?   Ask a Librarian

Collections   Service Areas   Classes & Tours   Arts

Library Catalog | Indexes & Abstracts | e-Journals & e-Books | e-Reference Sources | e-Newspapers & e-Proceedings | e-Resources | Catalogs of Other Libraries | Multi-search | Faculty liaisons & subject librarians

Organization Chart
IOWA STATE UNIVERSITY LIBRARY

Provost
Benjamin J. Allen

ISU Foundation

Director of Development
Karlene Jennings

Dean of the Library
Olivia Madison

Business Services
Shelley Hawkins

Human Resources
Pam Williams

Associate Dean
Research & Access
David Gregory

Associate Dean
Reference & Instruction
David Baldwin

Information
Technology Officer
Fred Gulden

Associate Dean
Collections & Technical Services
Kristin Gerhard

Circulation, Branch Facilities
& Horizon Support
Mary Jo Bergmann

Digital Access
Karen Lawson

Preservation
Hilary Seo

Special Collections
Tanya Zanish-Belcher

Stacks & Service Desks
Kathy Parsons

Social Sciences & Humanities
Rebecca Jackson

Science & Technology
Lorraine Pellack

Instruction Coordinator
Susan Vega Garcia

Desktop Infrastructure
Fred Gulden

Library Management Systems
Fred Gulden

Statewide Information
Network Online (SILO)
Alan Schmitz

Acquisitions
Janet Arcand

Cataloging
Lori Osmus

Collections Coordinator
Ed Goedeken

Printer-friendly version | e-Library entrance | Site Search | Site map | Top

Send questions or comments about this page
Last modified: Wednesday, 01-Sep-2004 14:02:22 CDT
Copyright © 2000-2005, Iowa State University. All rights reserved.

Otto G. Richter Library
Access & Delivery Services Organizational Chart

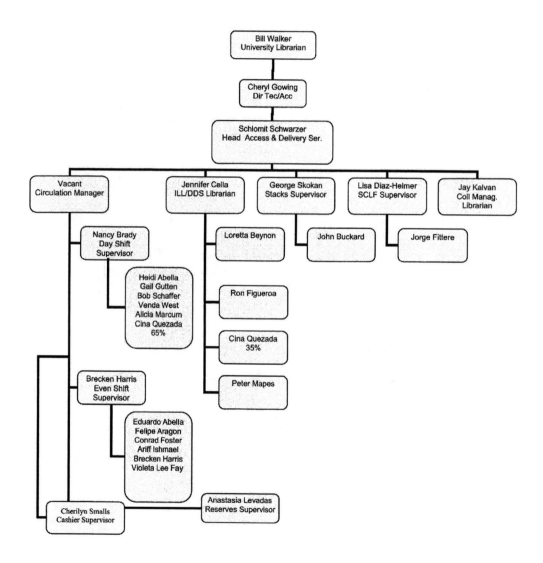

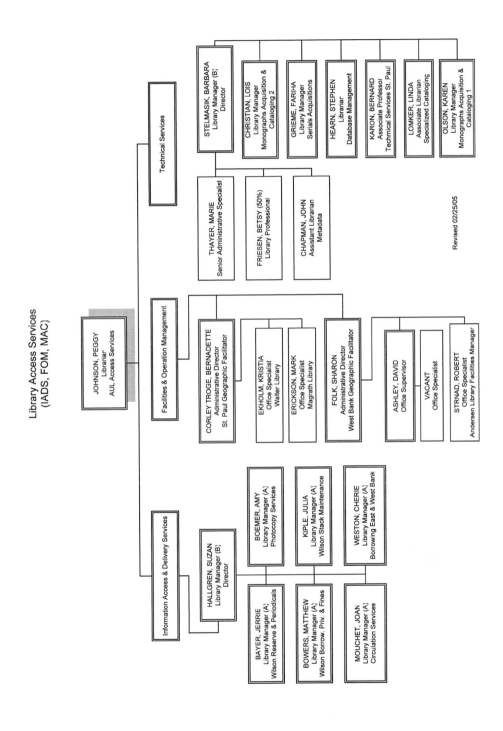

Library Access Services
(IADS, FOM, MAC)

JOHNSON, PEGGY
Librarian
AUL Access Services

Technical Services

STELMASIK, BARBARA
Library Manager (B);
Director

THAYER, MARIE
Senior Administrative Specialist

FRIESEN, BETSY (50%)
Library Professional

CHAPMAN, JOHN
Assistant Librarian
Metadata

CHRISTIAN, LOIS
Library Manager
Monographs Acquisition &
Cataloging 2

GRIEME, FARIHA
Library Manager
Serials Acquisitions

HEARN, STEPHEN
Librarian
Database Management

KARON, BERNARD
Associate Professor
Technical Services St. Paul

LOMKER, LINDA
Associate Librarian
Specialized Cataloging

OLSON, KAREN
Library Manager
Monographs Acquisition &
Cataloging 1

Revised 02/25/05

Facilities & Operation Management

CORLEY TROGE, BERNADETTE
Administrative Director
St. Paul Geographic Facilitator

EKHOLM, KRISTIA
Office Specialist
Walter Library

ERICKSON, MARK
Office Specialist
Magrath Library

FOLK, SHARON
Administrative Director
West Bank Geographic Facilitator

ASHLEY, DAVID
Office Supervisor

VACANT
Office Specialist

STRNAD, ROBERT
Office Specialist
Andersen Library Facilities Manager

Information Access & Delivery Services

HALLGREN, SUZAN
Library Manager (B);
Director

BOEMER, AMY
Library Manager (A);
Photocopy Services

BAYER, JERRIE
Library Manager (A);
Wilson Reserve & Periodicals

KIPLE, JULIA
Library Manager (A);
Wilson Stack Maintenance

BOWERS, MATTHEW
Library Manager (A);
Wilson Borrow. Priv. & Fines

WESTON, CHERIE
Library Manager (A);
Borrowing East & West Bank

MOUCHET, JOAN
Library Manager (A);
Circulation Services

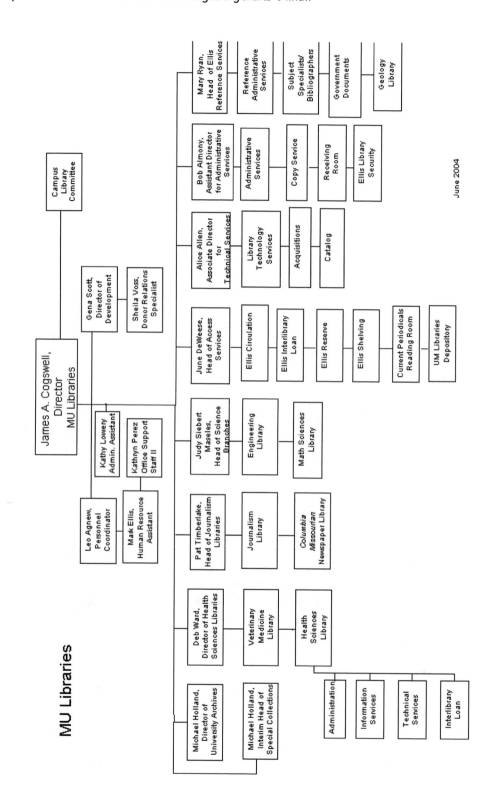

MU Libraries

June 2004

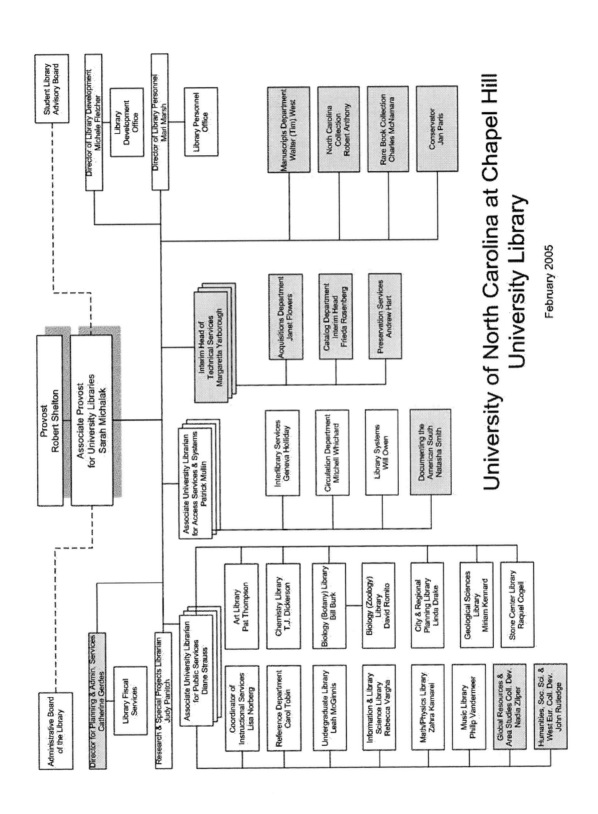

University of North Carolina at Chapel Hill
University Library

February 2005

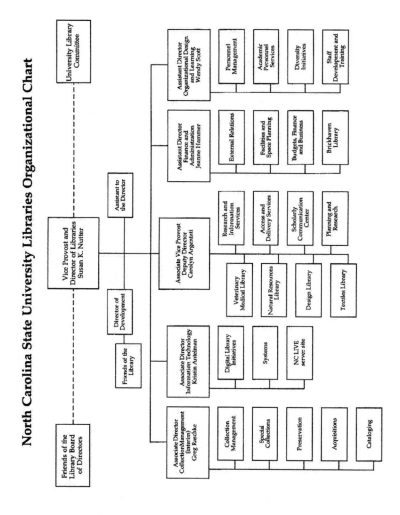

North Carolina State University Libraries Organizational Chart

ACCESS AND DELIVERY SERVICES

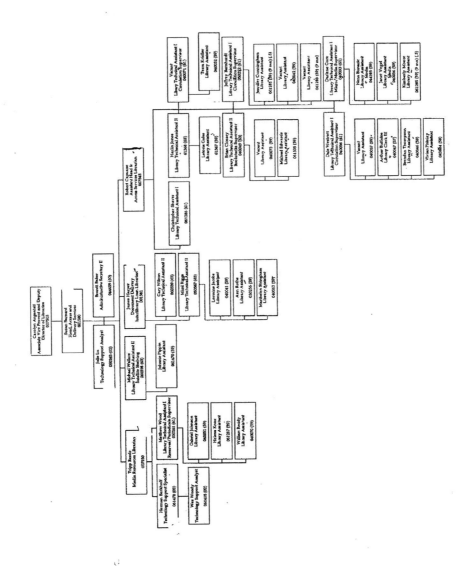

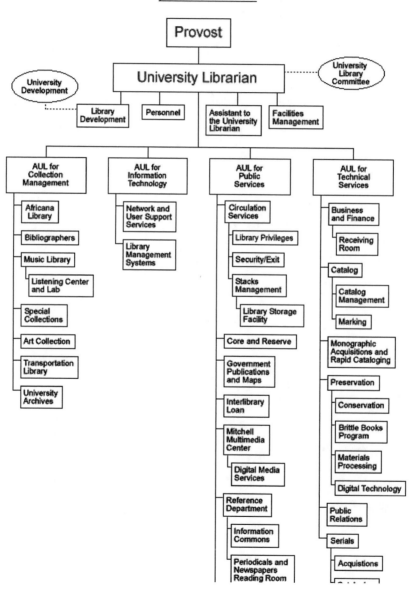

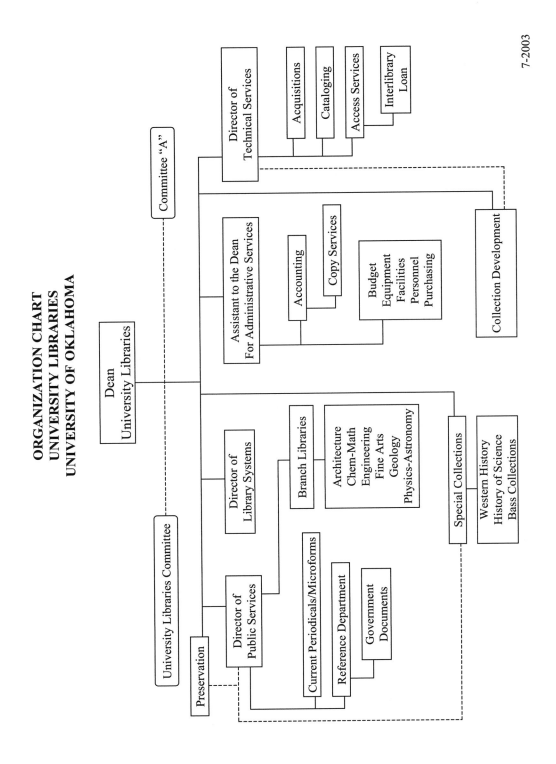

ORGANIZATION CHART
UNIVERSITY LIBRARIES
UNIVERSITY OF OKLAHOMA

7-2003

Dean
University Libraries

Committee "A"

University Libraries Committee

Director of Technical Services

Acquisitions

Cataloging

Access Services

Interlibrary Loan

Assistant to the Dean
For Administrative Services

Accounting

Copy Services

Budget
Equipment
Facilities
Personnel
Purchasing

Collection Development

Director of Library Systems

Branch Libraries

Architecture
Chem-Math
Engineering
Fine Arts
Geology
Physics-Astronomy

Special Collections

Western History
History of Science
Bass Collections

Preservation

Director of Public Services

Current Periodicals/Microforms

Reference Department

Government Documents

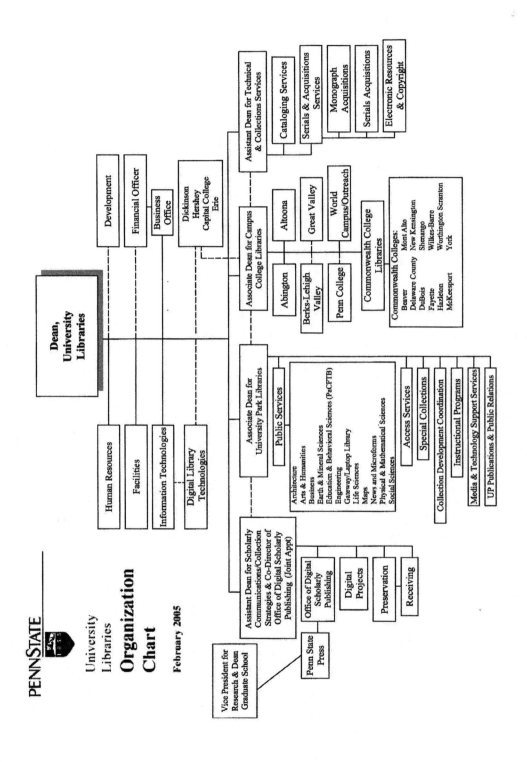

University
Libraries
**Organization
Chart**

February 2005

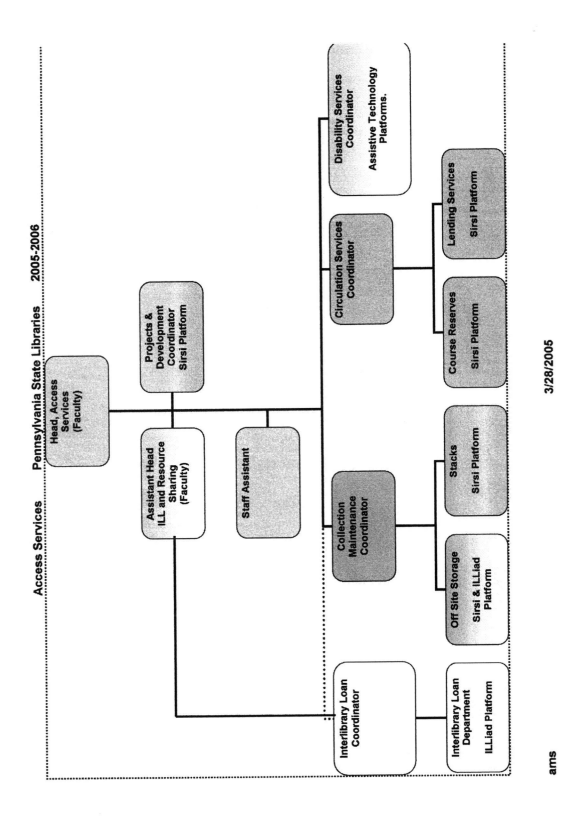

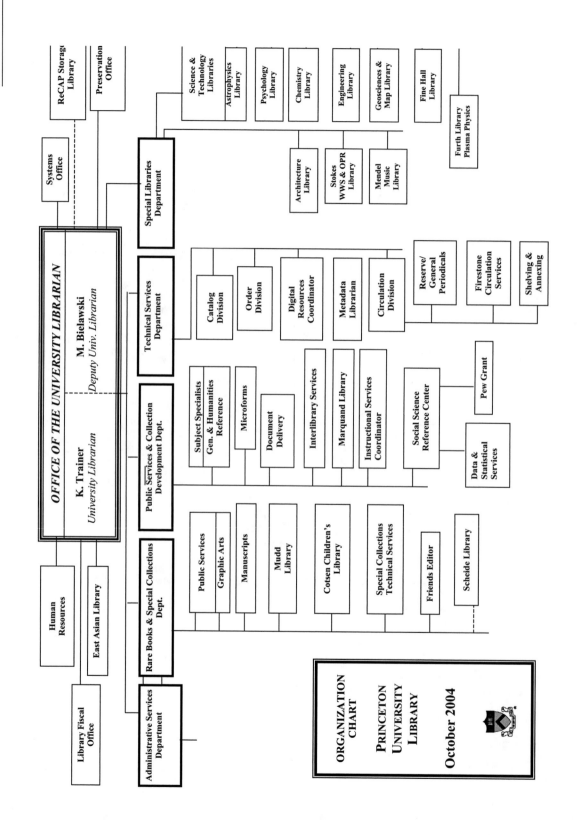

ORGANIZATION CHART

PRINCETON UNIVERSITY LIBRARY

October 2004

Technical Services Department

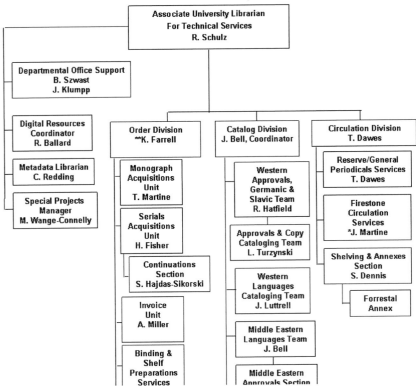

Purdue University Libraries

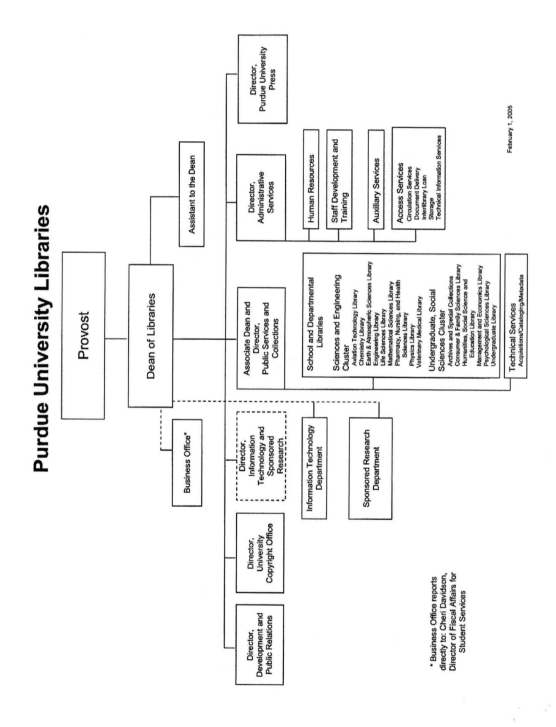

Provost

Dean of Libraries

Assistant to the Dean

Business Office*

Director, Development and Public Relations

Director, University Copyright Office

Director, Information Technology and Sponsored Research

Information Technology Department

Sponsored Research Department

Associate Dean and Director, Public Services and Collections

School and Departmental Libraries

Sciences and Engineering Cluster
Aviation Technology Library
Chemistry Library
Earth & Atmospheric Sciences Library
Engineering Library
Life Sciences Library
Mathematical Sciences Library
Pharmacy, Nursing, and Health Sciences Library
Physics Library
Veterinary Medical Library

Undergraduate, Social Sciences Cluster
Archives and Special Collections
Consumer & Family Sciences Library
Humanities, Social Science and Education Library
Management and Economics Library
Psychological Sciences Library
Undergraduate Library

Technical Services
Acquisitions/Cataloging/Metadata

Director, Administrative Services

Human Resources

Staff Development and Training

Auxiliary Services

Access Services
Circulation Services
Document Delivery
Interlibrary Loan
Storage
Technical Information Services

Director, Purdue University Press

February 1, 2005

* Business Office reports directly to: Cheri Davidson, Director of Fiscal Affairs for Student Services

Purdue University Libraries

ACCESS SERVICES ORGANIZATION

Sue Ward
Head, Access Services

L. Christie
TIS Operations Manager

V. McLaughlin
Lead Document Asst 4

L. Chadwell
Clerk

S. Barrett
Clerk

A. O'Donnell
Clerk

M. Dugan
TIS Information Specialist

D. Lanzalotto
Lead Clerk 4

F. Nemec
Clerk 3

A. Winks
Circ/Doc Del Coordinator

C. Richards
Lib. Asst 4

D. Heemstra
Lib Asst 4

C. Sagendorf
Lib Asst 4

Y-I. Kim
Lib Asst 4

M. Boeckman
Clerk 3

P. Killian
Clerk 3

C. McNeely
Clerk 3

B. Tarver
Clerk 3

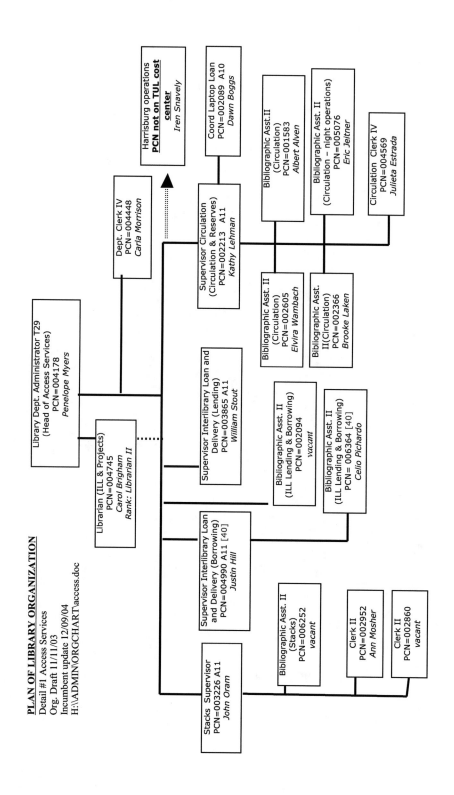

PLAN OF LIBRARY ORGANIZATION
Detail #1 Access Services
Org. Draft 11/11/03
Incumbent update 12/09/04
H:\ADMIN\ORGCHART\access.doc

Library Dept. Administrator T29
(Head of Access Services)
PCN=004178
Penelope Myers

Dept. Clerk IV
PCN=004448
Carla Morrison

Librarian (ILL & Projects)
PCN=004745
Carol Brigham
Rank: Librarian II

Harrisburg operations
PCN not on TUL cost center
Iren Snavely

Supervisor Circulation
(Circulation & Reserves)
PCN=002213 A11
Kathy Lehman

Coord Laptop Loan
PCN=002089 A10
Dawn Boggs

Bibliographic Asst. II
(Circulation)
PCN=001583
Albert Alven

Bibliographic Asst. II
(Circulation – night operations)
PCN=005076
Eric Jeitner

Circulation Clerk IV
PCN=004569
Julieta Estrada

Bibliographic Asst. II
(Circulation)
PCN=002605
Elvira Wambach

Bibliographic Asst.
II(Circulation)
PCN=002366
Brooke Laken

Supervisor Interlibrary Loan and
Delivery (Lending)
PCN=003865 A11
William Stout

Bibliographic Asst. II
(ILL Lending & Borrowing)
PCN=002094
vacant

Bibliographic Asst. II
(ILL Lending & Borrowing)
PCN= 006364 [40]
Celio Pichardo

Supervisor Interlibrary Loan
and Delivery (Borrowing)
PCN=004990 A11 [40]
Justin Hill

Stacks Supervisor
PCN=003226 A11
John Oram

Bibliographic Asst. II
(Stacks)
PCN=006252
vacant

Clerk II
PCN=002952
Ann Mosher

Clerk II
PCN=002860
vacant

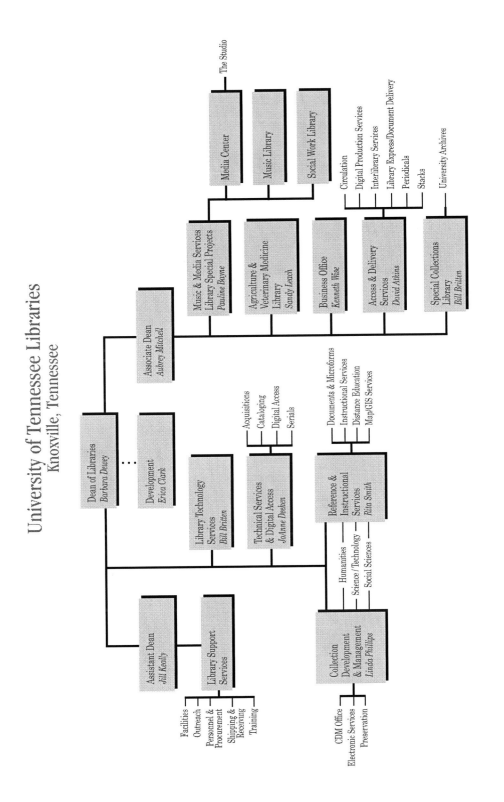

June 1, 2005

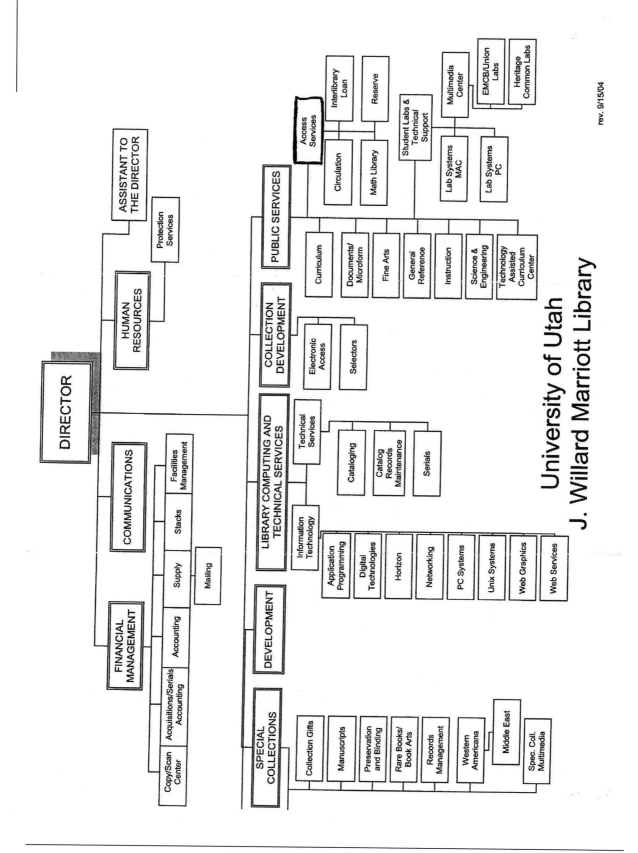

University of Utah
J. Willard Marriott Library

rev. 9/15/04

Virginia Tech University Libraries

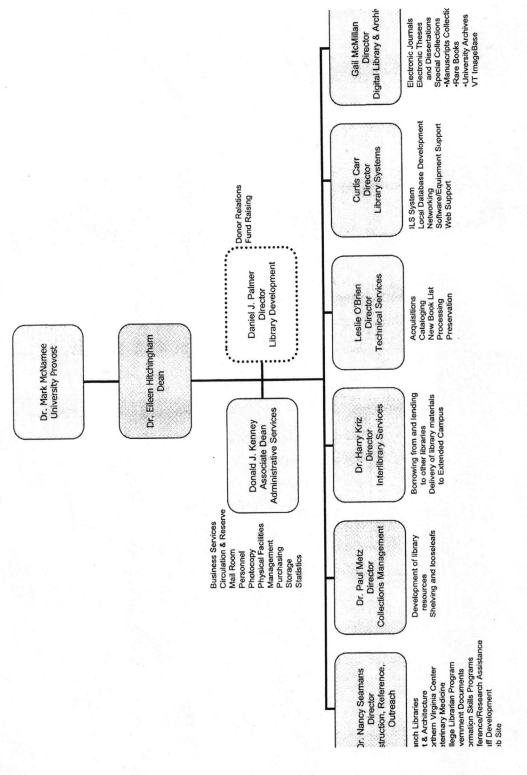

Dr. Mark McNamee
University Provost

Dr. Eileen Hitchingham
Dean

Daniel J. Palmer
Director
Library Development

Donor Relations
Fund Raising

Donald J. Kenney
Associate Dean
Administrative Services

Business Services
Circulation & Reserve
Mail Room
Personnel
Photocopy
Physical Facilities
Management
Purchasing
Storage
Statistics

Dr. Paul Metz
Director
Collections Management

Development of library
resources
Shelving and looseleafs

Dr. Harry Kriz
Director
Interlibrary Services

Borrowing from and lending
to other libraries
Delivery of library materials
to Extended Campus

Leslie O'Brien
Director
Technical Services

Acquisitions
Cataloging
New Book List
Processing
Preservation

Curtis Carr
Director
Library Systems

ILS System
Local Database Development
Networking
Software/Equipment Support
Web Support

Gail McMillan
Director
Digital Library & Archi

Electronic Journals
Electronic Theses
and Dissertations
Special Collections
•Manuscripts Collectic
•Rare Books
•University Archives
VT ImageBase

Dr. Nancy Seamans
Director
struction, Reference,
Outreach

anch Libraries
t & Architecture
orthern Virginia Center
eterinary Medicine
llege Librarian Program
vernment Documents
ormation Skills Programs
ference/Research Assistance
ff Development
eb Site

Research and Instructional Services
Updated 12/04

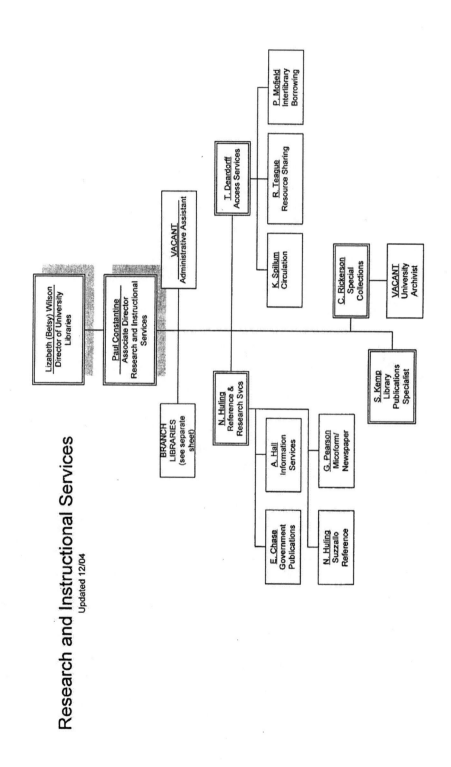

Lizabeth (Betsy) Wilson
Director of University Libraries

Paul Constantine
Associate Director
Research and Instructional Services

VACANT
Administrative Assistant

BRANCH LIBRARIES
(see separate sheet)

T. Deardorff
Access Services

P. Mofield
Interlibrary Borrowing

R. Teague
Resource Sharing

K. Spillum
Circulation

C. Rickerson
Special Collections

VACANT
University Archivist

S. Kemp
Library Publications Specialist

N. Huling
Reference & Research Svcs

A. Hall
Information Services

G. Pearson
Micoform/Newspaper

E. Chase
Government Publications

N. Huling
Suzzallo Reference

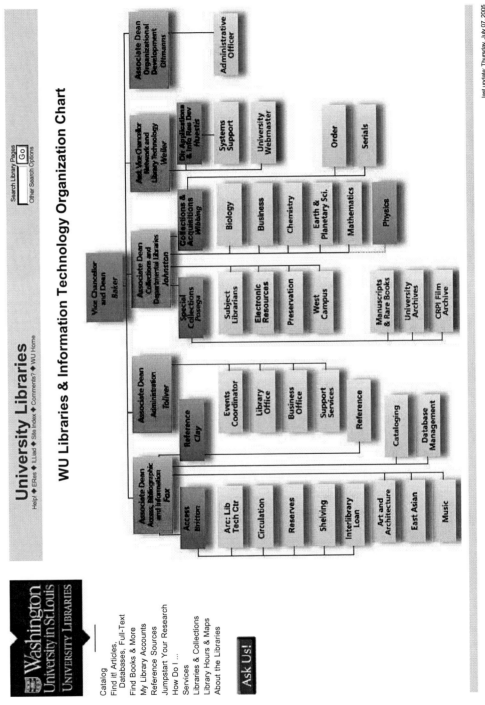

WU Libraries & Information Technology Organization Chart

Circulation Services

March 8, 2005

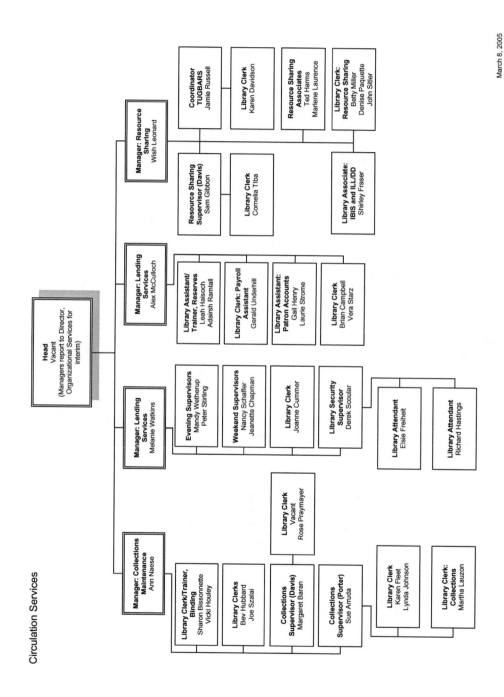

Head
Vacant
(Managers report to Director, Organizational Services for interim)

Manager: Collections Maintenance
Ann Naese

Library Clerk/Trainer, Binding
Sharon Bissonnette
Vicki Houley

Library Clerks
Bev Hubbard
Joe Szalai

Collections Supervisor (Davis)
Margaret Baran

Library Clerk
Vacant
Rose Praymayer

Collections Supervisor (Porter)
Sue Arruda

Library Clerk
Karen Fleet
Lynda Johnson

Library Clerk: Collections
Martha Lauzon

Manager: Lending Services
Melanie Watkins

Evening Supervisors
Mandy Wetherup
Peter Stirling

Weekend Supervisors
Nancy Schaffer
Jeanette Chapman

Library Clerk
Joanne Cummer

Library Security Supervisor
Derek Scoular

Library Attendant
Elsie Freiheit

Library Attendant
Richard Hastings

Manager: Lending Services
Alex McCulloch

Library Assistant/Trainer, Reserves
Leah Haisoch
Adairsh Ramlall

Library Clerk: Payroll Assistant
Gerald Underhill

Library Assistant: Patron Accounts
Gail Henry
Laurie Strome

Library Clerk
Brian Campbell
Vera Starz

Manager: Resource Sharing
Wish Leonard

Coordinator TUGBARS
Jamie Russell

Library Clerk
Karen Davidson

Resource Sharing Associates
Ted Harms
Marlene Laurence

Library Clerk: Resource Sharing
Betty Miller
Denise Paquette
John Sitler

Resource Sharing Supervisor (Davis)
Sam Gibbon

Library Clerk
Cornelia Tiba

Library Associate: IBIS and ILL/DD
Shirley Fraser

Circulation/Access Services Mission Statements

Home > Circulation

LIBRARY MENU

Find Articles
Find Books
Find Other Materials
Services
About the Library
Reservations

Circulation

Mission

Our goal is to facilitate faculty teaching and research, and to provide current and global resources for students. Our services are intended for the students, teachers and administrators of the Church Education System (excluding Seminary students), the Family History Library, the Church Historical Department, and all General Authorities of the Church of Jesus Christ of Latter-day Saints.

Location/Hours

The Circulation Desk is located on the third level (room 3443) of the Harold B. Lee Library. At the Circulation Desk patrons can check out library or reserve materials as well as paying off their fines. Other services provided include obtaining library pin numbers, returning course reserve items, and applying for Friends of the Library cards. To receive more information please contact us at 422-6061. Circulation Desk hours are:

	Fall / Winter Semesters	Spring / Summer Terms
Mon. - Fri.	7:00 am -12:00 am	7:00 am -10:00 pm
Saturday	8:00 am - 12:00 am	8:00 am - 10:00 pm

The Circulation Desk is closed on Tuesdays from 10:45-12:00 for Devotional.

Access Services Department

Mission and Goals

March 2004

Mission Statement

The General Library of the University of California, Davis, is a major educational and scholarly resource, operating as an integral part of the University while recognizing obligations to a wider public, particularly the people of California.

The mission of the Access Services Department is to preserve and provide access to the General Library's books, journals and other records of knowledge in support of University research, instruction, patient care, and community outreach. Through the interlibrary loan service, the Access Services Dept. provides access to research materials located throughout the United States and around the world. Some units of the Access Services Department have missions unique to Shields Library; other units have General Library missions.

Departmental Goals for Meeting Mission

1. To provide effective access to the open stack and reserve collections in Peter J. Shields Library and to UC Davis library materials stored offsite (e.g., Annex, NRLF).

2. To provide effective procedures for the off-site use of library materials to eligible borrowers.

3. To provide effective access to research materials located in other UC libraries, in libraries throughout the United States and world, and from information providers.

4. To provide a safe and secure and clean environment for patrons of the library and for materials housed in units of the General Library.

Where do Departmental Mission and Goals Intersect with General Library Unit Priorities (GLUP)?

1. Maintain the strength of library collections
   a. Provide effective building security to ensure the safety of the collections, staff, and library patrons.
   b. Provide an effective system to recover library materials that have been removed from the library.
   c. Continuously review eligibility standards for non-UC library users to ensure materials are available for primary users when needed.
   d. Promptly inform bibliographers when materials have been lost, so that they can be considered for replacement.
   e. Maintain a clean environment for staff and collections.

2. Provide effective access to scholarly resources in and through library facilities.
   a. Train staff and student employees to provide service and access.
   b. Maintain shelving turn-around-time standard.
   c. Maintain orderly shelves by shelf-reading.
   d. Maintain a clean environment for library materials and patrons.
   e. Provide study carrels and book lockers.
   f. Provide hold, recall, and routing service.
   g. Provide document delivery service.
   h. Provide interlibrary loan service.

3. Continually improve and monitor efficiency and scale of resource sharing
   a. Maintain accurate electronic records of requests initiated by library patrons for document delivery and interlibrary loan.
   b. Provide user-initiated electronic services whenever possible.
   c. Coordinate the development and expansion of resource sharing activities with other UC campuses using the most effective automated systems.

4. Provide state-of-the-art systems which make interaction with the library easier and more convenient
   a. Maintain accurate electronic records of library materials loaned to patrons.
   b. Provide user-initiated electronic services whenever possible.
   c. Provide easy to use document delivery and routing service.
   d. Maintain accurate records of library materials no longer available for use.
   e. Provide interlibrary loan and document delivery service management systems that make it easy to provide patrons with needed materials.
   f. Create temporary bibliographic records for materials that need to circulate to users.

5. Maintain and enhance an effective user assistance program
   a. Train staff and student employees to provide positive and helpful public service.
   b. Provide accurate information about library policies and practices to patrons through verbal, printed and web-based information.
   c. Maintain library service desk hours that meet patron needs.

ACCESS SERVICES

MISSION STATEMENT

In support of the research, teaching, and outreach mission of the University of Connecticut, Access Services provides:

- Long and short-term individual borrowing access to the Libraries' collections -- print, microforms, and multimedia – and access to equipment and facilities for use of non-print collections

- Individual electronic full text access to materials in high demand for University supported instruction

- Individual borrowing and photocopy access – in hard copy or via delivery to desktop -- to materials not owned by the Libraries

- Loan and photocopy access of library owned materials to other academic, public, and corporate libraries

- Instructional support for services offered

- Inventory control for the Libraries' circulating collections.

Access Services uses staff expertise and existing technologies to fulfill its mission in an environment responsive to client needs and supportive of client self-sufficiency.

UNIVERSITY OF MINNESOTA

UNIVERSITY OF MINNESOTA
LIBRARIES

INFORMATION ACCESS &
DELIVERY SERVICES

Home > Mission, Vision, Values

ABOUT IADS
Who We Are
Mission, Vision, Values
Organizational Chart
Functional Areas
Branch and Other Libraries
Councils and Groups
Staff Interviews

RESOURCES
Circulation Hours
Contacts
Coordinator Reports
Data and Statistics
E-mail Listserv
Forms and Templates
Macros
Meeting Notes
Planning and Goals
Policies
Procedures
Student Training Module

SERVICES
Security Monitor
Staffing Assistance

HELPFUL LINKS
Computer Tips
Copyright Info & Education
Copyright Staff Resources

MISSION, VISION, VALUES

OUR MISSION
The mission of the Information Access and Delivery Services Department is to provide efficient, effective, and innovative access to and delivery of information and materials to users in pursuit of knowledge, educational goals, research, teaching and scholarship.

WE ENVISION THAT
- The Libraries Environment is a welcoming environment
- Users receive what they need
- Users receive equitable levels of service whenever the libraries are open
- Users receive accurate and consistent information across the system
- Users are provided equitable access to information
- Users are provided with materials and/or information no matter the source equipment needs of both users and staff are met

WE VALUE
- Our users, their ideas, and suggestions
- Quality service for all
- Respect for individuals and their ideas
- Staff input and involvement in decision making
- A positive attitude
- Everyone working
- Continuous learning
- Creativity, risk taking, innovation and fun
- Courtesy for all
- Supporting each other and other teams

Trouble seeing the text? | Contact U of M | Privacy

Send comments to: iadsweb@umn.edu

Last Revision: July 22, 2005

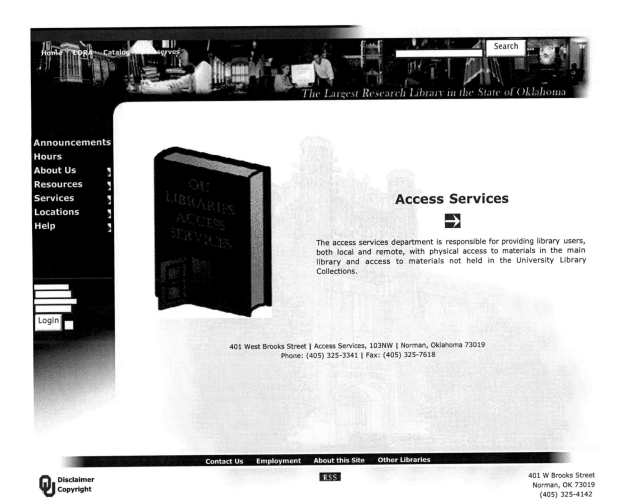

Home   CORA   Catalog   Reserves

Search

The Largest Research Library in the State of Oklahoma

Announcements
Hours
About Us
Resources
Services
Locations
Help

Login

Access Services

The access services department is responsible for providing library users, both local and remote, with physical access to materials in the main library and access to materials not held in the University Library Collections.

401 West Brooks Street | Access Services, 103NW | Norman, Oklahoma 73019
Phone: (405) 325-3341 | Fax: (405) 325-7618

Contact Us   Employment   About this Site   Other Libraries

RSS

Disclaimer
Copyright

401 W Brooks Street
Norman, OK 73019
(405) 325-4142

Technical Services Home   Cataloging Div   Circulation Div   Order Div

Circulation Division

Trevor A. Dawes, Circulation Services Director. Contact: 609.258.3231, tdawes@Princeton.EDU.

Joan Martine, Head, Firestone Circulation Services, and Assistant Division Head. Contact: 609.258.3244, jmartine@Princeton.EDU.

About the Circulation Services Division

The Circulation Services Division is responsible for providing direct services to Library patrons. Some of the tasks performed by staff in this Division include circulating material to patrons; processing reserve items and making them available to faculty and students; and maintaining the shelving accuracy of the Firestone Library and Forrestal Annex collections. The library patron is the focus of the mission and excellent service to patrons is the goal of all Circulation Services Division activities.

There are three units within the Division that make these services possible:

Firestone Circulation Services. Contact: **Joan Martine**, 609.258.3244, jmartine@Princeton.EDU

This unit is responsible for the basic circulation services in the Firestone Library. Here, library patrons may charge, renew or return library material. The Circulation staff is also responsible for locating items that are reported missing from the collection, and can assist patrons with other alternatives. Items that have been requested by patrons (such as through BorrowDirect, Interlibrary Loan, from the offsite storage facilities or from a Recall) are picked up at the Circulation Desk.

Reserve/General Periodicals Services. Contact: **Trevor A. Dawes**, 609.258.3231, tdawes@Princeton.EDU **or Lorie Cerbone Harding**, 609.258.3224, lcerbone@Princeton.EDU.

This unit is responsible for the receipt and processing of reserve requests from faculty and for making the requested items available to faculty and students. The Reserve/General Periodicals staff is also responsible for maintaining the current periodicals and newspaper collections in the Firestone Library.

Shelving & Annex Services. Contact: **Susan Dennis**. 609.258.3225, susan@Princeton.EDU.

This unit is responsible for the timely shelving and maintenance of the collections housed in the Firestone Library and the Forrestal Library Annex. Working with the other units in the Division, and in the Library, they ensure the availability and accessibility of the library's collections.

The Circulation Services Division:

- will employ skilled and competent staff, including student assistants, to provide all our services.
- will establish policies and procedures designed to provide optimal access to the collections.
- will maintain written policies and procedures covering internal operations and activities.
- will communicate with library staff and patrons alike on circulation matters of mutual concern.

Library Catalog | Research | **Hours** | Reserves | About the Library | Tulane University

Home > About The Library > Departments > **Access Services & Circulation**

+ NEED HELP? +

Services & staff

Library services

Department pages

Access Services &
Circulation

Architecture Library

Bibliographic
Services

Cataloging

CLUE

Collections

Digital Services

Gifts

Government
Documents

Interlibrary Loan

Latin American
Library

Maxwell Music Library

Microforms &
Newspapers

Reference &
Information Desk

Special Collections

Systems

Strategic plan

Staff & department
directory

Library policies

Academic honesty

Access Services & Circulation

The primary responsibility of the Access Services Department at the Howard-Tilton Library is to provide access to library material for our users. Our goal is to serve the Tulane University's faculty, students and staff as well as other patrons who wish to use our library. Access Services is responsible for the Circulation and Reserve Desk, Stacks Maintenance, Interlibrary Loan and Document Delivery, photocopiers, and network printing. Other services offered by Access Services are photocopying and material retrieval assistance services for patrons with physical disabilities, lost and found, locker and study carrel assignments, and collection security.

The Circulation and Reserve Desks are located in the lobby on the first floor. Interlibrary Loan and Document Delivery are located on the second floor of the library. The Centralized Sorting Area and book return bins are located immediately behind the Information Desk on the first floor. An overnight book drop is located to the right of the main entrance of the library.

» access services info

Location: Circulation Desk, First Floor, Howard-Tilton Memorial Library

Phone: 504.865.5689

Fax: 504.862.8967

Hours:
Current library hours

Contact: Felice Maciejewski

» related links

» Access services/circulation staff list
» Appeal fines & fees
» Borrowing policies
» Change of address
» Claims returned
» Exit control
» In-process request
» Interlibrary loan
» Offsite materials request
» Reserves
» Student employment

» related links: reciprocal borrowing programs

» LOUIS: The Louisiana Library Network
» LALINC

June 11, 2002

ACCESS SERVICES

The Marriott Library, Access Services Department, is a central part of the Public Services Division. Its goal is to provide users with friendly professional service in the areas of materials that we own and materials we don't own. Circulation consists of check out, holds, recalls, renewals, searches, lost books, claimed returns, fines and billing. Interlibrary loan obtains material the Marriott Library does not own from other libraries. The Math Library provides complete service to users in that area. Reserve has a growing collection of electronic reserve material that can be accessed on-line, as well as books and a paper collection that professors have requested for their students. Stacks/reshelving scours the building and book drops every hour to gather material needing to be checked in and reshelved. UTAD, Utah article delivery, is a fast fax based way to obtain articles not held in the Marriott Library. It is necessary to have access to a fax right now, but in the near future desk top delivery will be possible.

Circulation:
Location: East (3rd floor) and West(1st floor) Exits Marriott Library
Phone: 801-581-8203
Email: Circdept@library.utah.edu

Interlibrary Loan:
Location: 303 Marriott Library
Phone: 801-581-6010 Fax: 801-581-4882
Email: Ill-req@library.utah.edu

Math Library:
Location: 121 JWB
Phone: 801-581-6208

Reserve Desk:
Location: 1701 Marriott Library
Phone: 801-581-6049
Email: Reserve@library.utah.edu

Stacks/Reshelving:
Location: 205 Marriott Library
Phone: 801-581-6856

UTAD (Utah Article Delivery)
Location: 303 Marriott Library
Phone: 801-581-6010
Email: Utad@library.utah.edu

Circulation/Access Services Home Pages

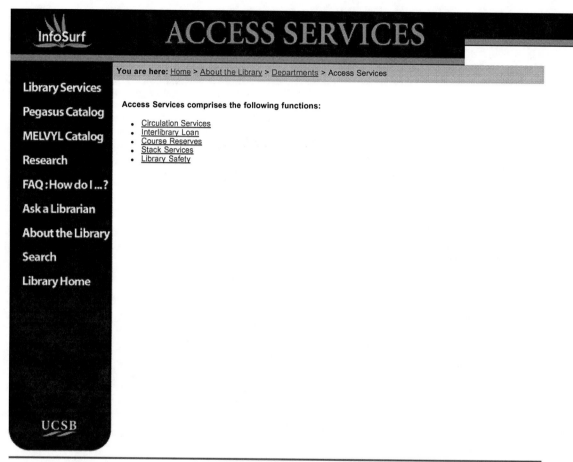

ACCESS SERVICES

InfoSurf

You are here: Home > About the Library > Departments > Access Services

Library Services

Pegasus Catalog

MELVYL Catalog

Research

FAQ : How do I ...?

Ask a Librarian

About the Library

Search

Library Home

UCSB

Access Services comprises the following functions:

- Circulation Services
- Interlibrary Loan
- Course Reserves
- Stack Services
- Library Safety

Comments: Eric Forte, Head.
Updated: 10/11/04 08:30:47

This is an official University of California Santa Barbara Libraries' web page. Please send comments to the Web Administrator.

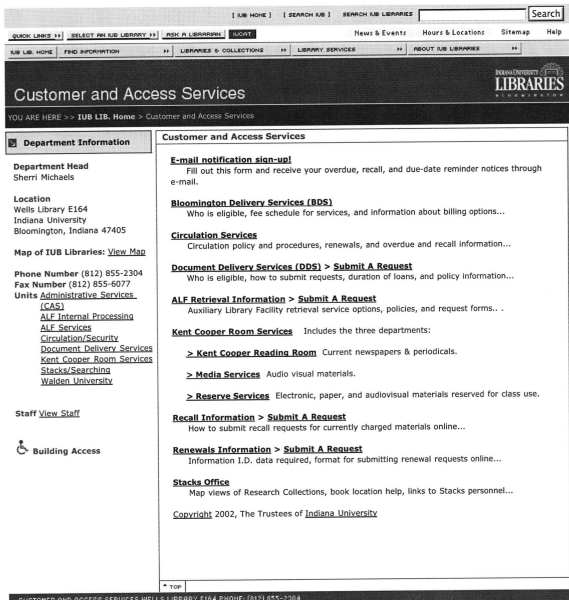

IUB Libraries: Customer and Access Services Home Page
10/24/05 12:52 PM

[IUB HOME]   [SEARCH IUB]   SEARCH IUB LIBRARIES | Search |

QUICK LINKS ▶▶   SELECT AN IUB LIBRARY ▶▶   ASK A LIBRARIAN   IUCAT
News & Events   Hours & Locations   Sitemap   Help

IUB LIB. HOME   FIND INFORMATION   ▶▶   LIBRARIES & COLLECTIONS   ▶▶   LIBRARY SERVICES   ▶▶   ABOUT IUB LIBRARIES   ▶▶

Customer and Access Services

INDIANA UNIVERSITY LIBRARIES BLOOMINGTON

YOU ARE HERE >> **IUB LIB. Home** > Customer and Access Services

Department Information

Department Head
Sherri Michaels

Location
Wells Library E164
Indiana University
Bloomington, Indiana 47405

Map of IUB Libraries: View Map

Phone Number (812) 855-2304
Fax Number (812) 855-6077
Units Administrative Services
(CAS)
ALF Internal Processing
ALF Services
Circulation/Security
Document Delivery Services
Kent Cooper Room Services
Stacks/Searching
Walden University

Staff View Staff

Building Access

Customer and Access Services

E-mail notification sign-up!
Fill out this form and receive your overdue, recall, and due-date reminder notices through e-mail.

Bloomington Delivery Services (BDS)
Who is eligible, fee schedule for services, and information about billing options...

Circulation Services
Circulation policy and procedures, renewals, and overdue and recall information...

Document Delivery Services (DDS) > Submit A Request
Who is eligible, how to submit requests, duration of loans, and policy information...

ALF Retrieval Information > Submit A Request
Auxiliary Library Facility retrieval service options, policies, and request forms.. .

Kent Cooper Room Services   Includes the three departments:

> **Kent Cooper Reading Room** Current newspapers & periodicals.

> **Media Services** Audio visual materials.

> **Reserve Services** Electronic, paper, and audiovisual materials reserved for class use.

Recall Information > Submit A Request
How to submit recall requests for currently charged materials online...

Renewals Information > Submit A Request
Information I.D. data required, format for submitting renewal requests online...

Stacks Office
Map views of Research Collections, book location help, links to Stacks personnel...

Copyright 2002, The Trustees of Indiana University

▲ TOP

CUSTOMER AND ACCESS SERVICES WELLS LIBRARY E164 PHONE: (812) 855-2304

INDIANA UNIVERSITY

http://www.libraries.iub.edu/index.php?pageId=279
Comments to libref@indiana.edu
Copyright 2001 - 2005, The Trustees of Indiana University
IUB Libraries Privacy Policy

Quick Links

*ACCESS
SERVICES HOME*

*DESCRIPTION OF
SERVICES*

*MAIN LIBRARY
DEPARTMENTS*
*CIRCULATION
SERVICES*
*RESERVE
SERVICES*
*INTERLIBRARY
LOAN*
MEDIA SERVICES

BOOKSTACKS

*CIRCULATION
POLICIES*
*Long Term Loans:
Main Stacks
Materials
Branch Materials
Short Term Loans:
Journals, Reserve,
etc.
Fines and Bills
Search Services
My Account*

REQUIRED ID

*CIRCULATING
COLLECTIONS*

*ACCESS
SERVICES
DOCUMENTATION*

*e-REQUEST
FORMS*

CONTENTS

CONTACT US

THE UNIVERSITY OF IOWA

LIBRARIES

Access Services

Access Services at the University of Iowa Libraries consists of Circulation, Reserve, Interlibrary Loan, Bookstacks and Media Services.

Circulation and Reserve services are located in the Main Library, Hardin Library and at each branch library.

Interlibrary Loan offices are located in the Main Library and the Hardin Library for the Health Sciences.

The Libraries Bookstacks and Media Services units are located in the Main Library.

The Distance Education Librarian, Stephen Dew, has his office in the Main Library. Distance education students and faculty can contact him directly at:
Phone 319 335-5069 or e-mail stephen-dew@uiowa.edu

Click here to see further information on individual Access Services activities

Main Library Access Services Locations:

Main Library Bookstacks (4th floor Main Library)

Circulation Services (1st floor south, Main Library)

Main Library Interlibrary Loan (1st floor south, Main Library)

Media Services (1st floor, Main Library)

Main Library Reserve Services (1st floor south, Main Library)

Hardin Library Web Pages and Branch Library Web Pages

Art Library	335-3089	lib-art@uiowa.edu
Biological Services Library	335-3083	lib-biology@uiowa.edu
Marvin A. Pomerantz Business Library	335-3077	lib-bus@uiowa.edu
Chemistry Library	335-3085	lib-chem@uiowa.edu

Libraries & Collections ⬍ Go

Keyword (use and, or, not) ⬍ Catalog Search search

How Do I...? | Hours | Catalog | Article Databases | E-Journal Finder

Davis Circulation-Home Page
Phone: 962-1053 | <u>Directions</u> | <u>Hours</u> | <u>Staff Contacts</u>

The Circulation Department is responsible for checking out and reshelving books, managing the main stacks, maintaining information on books in circulation, paging books from the Annex area in Wilson Library, assigning graduate carrels, accepting applications for faculty studies, and circulating laptops and wireless cards.

Circulation

Borrower Information
Loan Policies
Charges, Fines, & Fees
Laptop & Wireless Services
Book Requests

Resources

Carrels & Faculty Studies
Group Studies
Photocopiers
Coin Operated Lockers

Online Forms

Email Notification Application
Storage Request
Recalls & Holds

Home | Material Locations | Loan Policies | Fines | Laptops | Book Requests | Carrels | Group Studies
| Photocopiers | Lockers | Email Notifications | Storage Requests | Recall Requests | Library Home | UNC Home

Comments or questions: Marlin Murrell
URL: http://www.lib.unc.edu/circ/index.html
This page was last updated Monday, July 18, 2005.

Knight Library Access Services Department

1299 University of Oregon
Eugene, OR 97403-1299

(541) 346-3065 Circulation
(541) 346-3067 Reserves and Videos
(541) 346-1919 Current Periodicals
(541) 346-1901 Copiers

ecirc@darkwing.uoregon.edu

| Library Home |

- **Borrowing materials**
- **Course Reserves**
- **Summit Borrowing**
- **On site borrowing at other Libraries**
- **Oregon Card**
- **About your library account**
- **Login to your account**
- **Current Periodicals**
- **Current Newspapers**
- **Videos**
- **Copiers**

STAFF

Shirien Chappell, Head, 541.346-1914, chappell@darkwing.uoregon.edu

Circulation / Reserves and Videos

- Laura Willey, Supervisor 541.346-1915, lwilley@uoregon.edu
- Rick Peterson, Student Coordinator, Assistant to Unit Supervisor 541.346-1918 rpeterso@darkwing.uoregon.edu
- Dave Baker, Electronic Reserves Clerk 541.346-0753 dbaker2@darkwing.uoregon.edu
- Jen Lindsey, Billing Coordinator 541.346-1916 jfrog@darkwing.uoregon.edu
- Nancy Loya, Special Processes Clerk 541.346-0760 nwloya@darkwing.uoregon.edu
- Michelle Page, Search Clerk 541.346-0754 rpage@darkwing.uoregon.edu
- Matt Mensik, Video Clerk 541.346-1969 mmensik@darkwing.uoregon.edu
- Vonda Welty, Patron Database Clerk 541.346-1917 vwelty@darkwing.uoregon.edu
- Student Assistants (30 part time student assistants)

Current Periodicals & Stacks

- Shelia Stigall, Supervisor, 541.346-0759 sstigall@darkwing.uoregon.edu
- Neil Wilson, Student Supervisor/Newspaper Coordinator, Assistant to Unit Supervisor 541.346-1861 nwilson@darkwing.uoregon.edu
- Jimmy Murray, Lending Coordinator 541.346-0756 jmurray2@darkwing.uoregon.edu
- Erika Rivera, UO Summit Lending Coordinator 541.346-0758 erivera@darkwing.uoregon.edu
- Blake Scott, Evening Supervisor 541.346-0755 bscott@darkwing.uoregon.edu
- Liesl Vorderstrasse, Evening Supervisor 541.346-1936 liesl@darkwing.uoregon.edu
- Student Assistants (65 part time student assistants)

Copiers

- Stephen Issac, Copiers Coordinator, 541.346-0706 saisaac@darkwing.uoregon.edu

http://libweb.uoregon.edu/acs_svc/index.html
Last revision: August 15, 2005 by sc
Shirien Chappell, University of Oregon Libraries

credits

University of Oregon Libraries | Eugene, OR 97403-1299

THE UNIVERSITY of TENNESSEE | **University Libraries**

University Links ▼   A-Z Index / WebMail / Dept. Directory   Enter searc | Library Site Search ▼ 🔵

Access and Delivery Services, *Hodges Library*

Libraries Home

Library Catalog

Databases

Forms

Help

Services

Branches

Libraries A to Z

AskUs.Now!

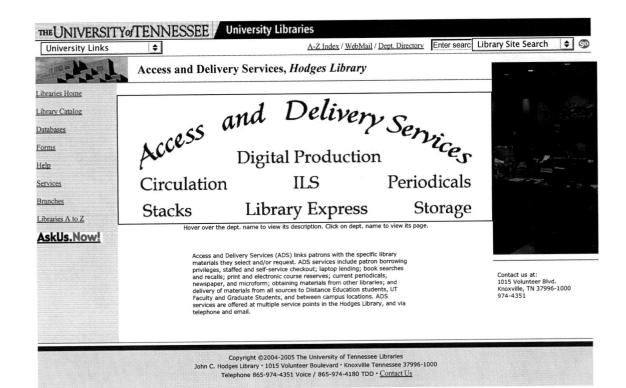

Access and Delivery Services

Digital Production

Circulation   ILS   Periodicals

Stacks   Library Express   Storage

Hover over the dept. name to view its description. Click on dept. name to view its page.

Access and Delivery Services (ADS) links patrons with the specific library materials they select and/or request. ADS services include patron borrowing privileges, staffed and self-service checkout; laptop lending; book searches and recalls; print and electronic course reserves; current periodicals, newspaper, and microform; obtaining materials from other libraries; and delivery of materials from all sources to Distance Education students, UT Faculty and Graduate Students, and between campus locations. ADS services are offered at multiple service points in the Hodges Library, and via telephone and email.

Contact us at:
1015 Volunteer Blvd.
Knoxville, TN 37996-1000
974-4351

WASHINGTON STATE UNIVERSITY

World Class. Face to Face.

CAMPUSES   WSU HOME   WSU SEARCH   myWSU

THE LIBRARIES

Griffin Catalog / Article Indexes/E-Journals / Your Record/Renewals

Libraries HOME
Search/Site Map
Hours/Phone
Contact Us
Ask a Question
Interlibrary Loans
Subject Resources
Reference Shelf
Classes & Handouts
Assistive Technology
About WSU Libraries
  Services
  Policies
  Departments
New Books
Libraries FAQ
News/Exhibits/Events
Other Library Catalogs
Giving to the Libraries

The Libraries - Your Information & Resources Gateway

ACCESS SERVICES

Each library in the WSU Libraries system has its own Circulation Desk where library materials may be checked out. Circulation staff check in and reshelve books as returned, recall books that have been requested by others, search for missing items, maintain the Reserve Collection, oversee fines and monitor the security system.

- Checking out material
- Loan periods
- Renewals
- Request Item
- Recalls for material already checked out
- Snags or missing items
- Materials on reserve
- Overdue notices
- Fines
- Griffin PIN
- Guest users
- Security system
- Contacting circulation

CHECK OUT: To check out an item, present it with your valid WSU identification card at the Circulation Desk. After the book has been checked out, it will be desensitized to permit it to pass through the security gates. Faculty members who intend to have teaching or research assistants check out material for them should inquire about proxy cards at the Circulation Desk. Applications for guest library user privileges are available at each library's Circulation Desk.

For most materials, the library circulation system operates by computer. You may determine where items are kept and whether or not they are currently checked out by using public access computers located in all WSU Libraries. Instructions for use of the online catalog are avilable at each library. Some items, such as journals, are checked out manually. If you do not find an item on the shelf or listed in the computer system, ask at the Circulation Desk.

LOAN PERIODS: The regular loan period for most books is 30 days for undergraduate students and staff, and one semester for graduate students and faculty. Books requested from Summit have a 21 day circulation period. All materials checked out, excluding Summit items, are subject to recall after two weeks if needed by another borrower. Circulation periods for other materials, such as journals and some books, are determined by the individual library. Since circulation periods vary, always be sure to notice when an item is due at the time you check it out.

RENEWALS: If material is needed beyond the original loan period it must be renewed. Material may be renewed at a WSU Libraries Circulation Desk, by telephone or in person. Additionally, you may renew materials online through the Griffin catalog, using the View Your Records/Renewals/PIN button. Summit items checked out through Griffin may be renewed once for a 21-day period. Note that recalls placed on items could prohibit renewals (See RECALLS below.)

REQUEST ITEM: Using the "Request Item" button in the Griffin catalog and the "Request This Item" link in the statewide Summit catalog, you can request that items be delivered to the WSU Libraries Circulation Desk of your choice. In the Griffin catalog, click on the Request Item button when viewing a record. You must enter your name (last name is acceptable), WSU ID number, and a Griffin PIN to use online requesting. When submitting the request, you will be prompted to select an item pickup location.

You can search the Summit catalog by clicking on the "Search Summit" link on the introductory Griffin screen or by clicking on the "Search Summit" button available on any search results screen in Griffin. Both the Institutional Holdings Display and the Detailed Holdings Display screens in Summit provide "Request This Item" links. As with Griffin Request Item, you must enter your name, WSU ID number, with a leading zero, and Griffin PIN and select a WSU Libraries pickup location.

RECALLS: If you need a book which is already checked out to another borrower, you may "recall" it. You may recall a book via Griffin. When you are in Griffin at the record for the item you want, click on the Request Item button and complete the form. This recalls the book - sets in motion a request to the person who has the item to return it to the library so someone else (you in this case) can use it. You may also ask circulation staff to "recall" the item for you.

A recall may be requested any time; however, each person is permitted to keep borrowed books a minimum of 2 weeks. Once a recall is initiated on a book, the borrower is notified that another person is waiting and given five days to return the material to the library. When the material is returned, the person requesting it is notified that the material is waiting at the Circulation Desk. Books that have been recalled are subject to higher than normal fees if not returned by the new due date.

SNAGS: If an item is not checked out and you cannot find it on the shelf, please report it to the Circulation Desk. A "snag" reported to the Circulation Desk initiates a systematic search for the missing item by members of the

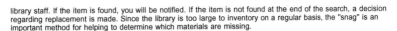

library staff. If the item is found, you will be notified. If the item is not found at the end of the search, a decision regarding replacement is made. Since the library is too large to inventory on a regular basis, the "snag" is an important method for helping to determine which materials are missing.

RESERVE: Heavily used items and those requested by instructors for assigned class reading are kept on Reserve. In Holland/New Library, the Reserve Desk is located in Media Materials & Reserves on the Ground Floor. Items on reserve in Brain Education and Owen Science & Engineering Libraries are kept at Circulation. Items are available upon request as long as the call number from the Griffin Online Catalog and a valid WSU ID are supplied. Architecture, Fischer Agricultural Sciences and Health Sciences Libraries have "open" reserve collections which patrons can use directly without asking. Because of the demand for these items, loan periods are shortened, fine rates are higher, and materials cannot be "recalled."

OVERDUE NOTICES: Library materials become overdue if not returned by the due date. An overdue notice is usually sent as a courtesy reminder. *You* are responsible for returning borrowed items *on time* whether or not an overdue notice is received.

FINES: The fine system is used by the library to encourage maximum accessibility to materials. Different kinds of materials have different check out periods and different fine schedules. These loan periods and fine schedules are published in the *WSU Library Policies, Rules and Regulations* (WAC 504-40) which is avilable at all Circulation and Reference Desks. Fines accrue during all hours the library is open, including holidays. Fine invoices are mailed directly to the borrower. Payments may be made in person or by mail to the Office of the Controller, WSU, Pullman, WA 99164-1039. Questions or problems about a particular fine may be directed to the Circulation Desk from which the item was borrowed.

GRIFFIN PIN: You must have a Griffin PIN, or *Personal Identification Number*, to submit requests via the Griffin and Summit catalogs and to view your patron record in Griffin. See this help document for more detailed information on Griffin PINs.

GUEST USERS: Consistent with the Washington Administrative Code (504-40-020), Washington state residents who are not affiliated with Washington State University may use Libraries resources and services, and borrow library materials. Individuals 16 years of age or older may apply for an off-campus borrower card at any WSU Libraries Circulation Desk. Acceptable forms of ID that can be used for signing up for a borrower card include identification from a federal agency, state agency, or another academic institution.

Guest users may request WSU Libraries items to be delivered to a WSU Libraries Circulation Desk by filling out a Search Request Card and submitting it to a Circulation Desk. Guest users may not recall items currently checked out.

SECURITY SYSTEM: To ensure that library materials are properly checked out when they leave the library, an electronic security system has been installed. When a book or journal is checked out, the Circulation attendant desensitizes it, allowing it to pass through the security gate. Material which has not been desensitized will cause the alarm to sound and the security gate to lock. Occasionally a non-library item will trigger the security system. Whatever the cause, when the alarm sounds, all books and packages will be examined to make certain that library materials have been properly checked out. If non-circulating materials, e.g., reference items, or current journals are found, a written report of the incident will be filed with the Student Affairs Office and WSU Police Services.

CONTACTING CIRCULATION: You can telephone the circulation desk at the appropriate library:

Architecture Library, 335-4967;
Brain Education Library, 335-1591;
Fischer Agricultural Sciences Library, 335-2266;
Health Sciences Library, 335-9556.
Holland/New Library, 335-9671;
Owen Science and Engineering Library, 335-2672;

Contact us: libweb@wsu.edu 509-335-9671 | Accessibility | Copyright | Policies
WSU Libraries, Washington State University, Pullman, WA, 99164-5610 USA

Last updated on Wednesday September 14th, 2005.
http://www.wsulibs.wsu.edu/general/circ.htm

University of
Waterloo   home   search   groups   depts   contacts   bookings   lib info   news   tools

UW Library Staff Web

▶ **Home**

▶ **Staff Contacts**

▶ **Guiding Principles**

▶ **Staff Only Site**

CIRCULATION SERVICES

Circulation Services staff are located in both Davis and Porter Libraries.

With a staff complement of 34 full-time and approximately 60 casual (i.e. part-time) staff, Circulation Services is the largest department in the UW Library.

The principal areas of departmental responsibility are:

Lending Services -- based on a lending policy shared by the TriUniversity Group of Libraries (TUG) and supported by an automated system, TRELLIS. Services include:

- circulation of library materials
- maintaining borrowers' records
- recalling or searching for circulating or missing material
- notifying borrowers of overdue material
- collection of late fees and replacement charges
- processing material for the Reserves collection
- ensuring that all Library material leaving Porter and Davis is properly charged out
- ensuring that the facilities are secure responding to situations involving a threat to the personal safety or reasonable comfort of anyone in the buildings

Collections -- includes :

- shelving material newly received or returned from circulation
- maintaining material on the shelves in an orderly fashion   [Top of page]
- shifting collections as necessary
- ensuring that space is available where needed for growing collections
- processing material to be transferred to the TUG cooperative storage facility (i.e. the Annex)
- processing material to be bound
- conduction inventories of the collections

Resource Sharing -- includes:

- providing a book and article retrieval service to TUG borrowers
- retrieving and sending material to Distance Education students and co-op students on workterm

In carrying out these responsibilities, Circulation Services staff work closely with other library staff, our TUG partners, other campus libraries/resource centres, and the University at large.

Job Descriptions

POSITION DESCRIPTION

DATE: January, 2001

DEPARTMENT: Access Services

TITLE: Head, Access Services and Interlibrary Loan

GENERAL SUMMARY:

Head of Access Services and Interlibrary Loan/Document Delivery Services (ILL/DDS) is an Academic Professional with administrative appointment who reports to the Associate Dean for Library Services. Responsible for providing management and leadership for the department, including directing, staffing, coordinating, reporting, planning, organizing and budgeting. Access Services includes the circulation, filing and/or shelf maintenance of print and alternative format materials and user assistance related to these materials in both Hayden and Noble Libraries. Also included are functions related to course reserve, electronic reserve, security for University Libraries, storage of library materials and the University Libraries Access to Disability Accommodation service. Interlibrary Loan/Document Delivery includes the lending of ASU-owned materials to other libraries and the acquisition of materials not owned by ASU for the use of the campus community as well as rapid delivery of these materials. Contributes to the management of the University Libraries. Works independently, with vision and initiative, taking risks while using sound judgment.

ESSENTIAL FUNCTIONS:

1. Plans, develops, implements, and monitors the policies, programs and services for Access Services and ILL/DDS. In consultation with appropriate library and faculty advisory committees, coordinates these activities with the priorities, objectives and policies of the University Libraries and with user needs.

2. Coordinates the provision of library collection access and document delivery services on the main campus and with those services offered by ASU campuses and locations away from the main campus. Serves as liaison with librarians and staff at these locations.

3. Maintains open channels of communication with the following constituencies to insure that user needs are considered and served, that services and planning are coordinated, and that policies are applied and implemented consistently with:

    a. Faculty and students, particularly those of the academic departments served by the University Libraries;

    b. Lending and borrowing libraries and institutions;

   c. Departmental staff, to foster an understanding of the department's roles in fulfilling the mission and goals of the University Libraries;

   d. Library administrators and personnel, as appropriate;

   e. Library users who present questions, complaints, or appeals;

   f. Various University offices that oversee benefits, privileges, and financial accounts pertaining to faculty, staff, students, and local community users.

4. Hires, trains, supervises, develops and evaluates staff. Directs the hiring, training, supervision, development and evaluation of other department staff. Initiates and directs disciplinary actions as appropriate and in accordance with university and library policy and guidelines.

5. Analyzes the activities, and processes of the department. Makes data-driven recommendations for continuous improvement.

6. Prepares budget analysis recommendations as well as reports, studies and/or surveys as required.

7. Designs and implements outreach programs to ILL/DDS customers. Markets and provides instruction in programs and services.

8. Takes a leadership role in resource-sharing programs and procedures in local, state, and national programs. Advises Library Administration and Collection Development of developments in resource-sharing programs and networks. Represents the ASU Libraries in planning for statewide, regional, national or international interlibrary loan services.

9. Takes a leadership role in defining library use policies such as loan policies, circulation privileges and information assistance.

10. Monitors and enforces copyright and licensing agreements as appropriate to ILL/DDS and Reserve Services.

11. Provides bibliographic expertise and oversight for interpretation and verification of information requests.

11. Coordinates access and security policies and procedures for University Libraries and campus units. Supervises library security personnel to maintain appropriate levels of security throughout the University Libraries.

12. Contributes to the management of the University Libraries by participating in the development of recommendations for coordination, and interpretation of library-wide

policies, plans and programs. Participates in Administrative Council, Library Services Council, Strategic Planning Council, library committees and meetings as appropriate.

13. Engages in professional development and service activities as required by the criteria for the promotion and continuing appointment of academic professionals in the University Libraries.

12. Performs other non-essential related responsibilities as assigned.

QUALIFICATIONS:

Required:

- American Library Association accredited Master of Library/Information Sciences degree.
- Five years' experience as a librarian in an academic, research, public or special library, including experience in public service.
- Demonstrated successful managerial skills, including the supervision of staff.
- Excellent communication skills.
- Demonstrated interpersonal skills, including the ability to work with students, faculty and staff.
- Ability to work within an organization that emphasizes staff collaboration, including working in small group and team environments.
- Demonstrated ability to plan, implement and evaluate library programs and services using data analysis.
- Knowledge of information literacy, electronic information systems and resources relevant to the academic and/or research library environment.
- Demonstrated interest in professional activity related to promotion and continuing status criteria.

PREFERRED:

- Experience as a reference librarian in an academic research library.
- Experience with electronic bibliographic utilities such as OCLC, RLIN.
- Knowledge of trends in interlibrary loan and document delivery.
- Knowledge of principles and processes for providing outstanding customer service including quality service standards, customer satisfaction evaluation, and related attributes.

EMPLOYEE SIGNATURE   DATE   SUPERVISOR SIGNATURE DATE

Effective date: November 15, 2004

UNIVERSITY OF CALIFORNIA, DAVIS
GENERAL LIBRARY

STATEMENT OF PRIMARY* RESPONSIBILITIES

NAME:_____

DEPARTMENT:____Access Services_____

PAYROLL TITLE:__Librarian_____

WORKING TITLE:__Head, Access Services Dept._____

NAMES & PAYROLL TITLES OF THOSE WHOSE WORK IS REVIEWED:

> Library Assistant V
> Library Assistant IV-S
> Library Assistant IV-S
> Library Assistant III-S
> Library Assistant II

REVIEW INITIATOR'S NAME: REVIEW INITIATOR'S PAYROLL TITLE:

Associate University Librarian for Administrative Services

DESCRIPTION OF RESPONSIBILITIES ASSIGNED IN COMMON:

Under the general direction of the Associate University Librarian for Administrative Services, responsible for overall administration of the Access Services Department, including formulation of departmental policies and procedures; development of new programs and services to improve the quality of public services provided to library users; planning of departmental facilities and equipment; maintenance of statistics relating to services; preparation of annual reports and departmental correspondence; resolution or referral of patron complaints.

Responsible for selection, supervision of training, evaluation, determination of work assignments, and responsibilities of employees. Consults with staff on personnel problems, grievances, etc. and refers to higher administrative level when advisable.

Responsible for maintenance of communication within the department through meetings and memoranda; representation of the department at the Library Management Council and on the library committees; liaison between the department and the Library Administration; interpretation of Library and University procedures to Department staff, maintenance of communication with other Library departments.

DESCRIPTION OF UNIQUE RESPONSIBILITIES:

Supervises directly or indirectly, Circulation Services, Interlibrary Loan, Reserve Services, Stack Services, Library Security, and the Mail Services.

Permanent chair of the Access Services Group and UC Davis representative to the SOPAG Resource Sharing Committee.

Participates in planning for access services-related functions in automated library systems.

As designated, represents the Library and University in other forums related to department functions.

SIGNATURE   SIGNATURE OF REVIEW INITIATOR

_____   _____

DATE:_____   DATE:_____

*The Statement of Primary Responsibilities describes the librarian's specific functions to be judged under the first criterion, "Professional competence and quality of service within the library," as explained in APM 210-4.e.3.a.

STATEMENT OF DUTIES AND RESPONSIBILITIES
Librarian Series

INCUMBENT IDENTIFICATION

Name: _____   Date of Initial Appointment: _____

Academic Rank/Step: _____   Current Date: _____

Primary Supervisor: _____   Secondary Supervisor: _____

Functional JobTitle: _____   Direct Supervision of: _____

SUMMARY OF DUTIES AND RESPONSIBILITIES
(Outline of major duties associated with this position)

A. HEAD OF ACCESS SERVICES

Under the direction of the AUL, Information and Research Services, is responsible for the organization, administration, and management of the Access Services Department, including circulation, reserve book services, stacks services, remote storage, current periodicals, interlibrary loan and document delivery, and safety and security. Supervises, trains, and evaluates staff in the provision of responsible services and is responsible for establishing goals and objectives, ongoing planning and direction, and works to continually improve services. Responsible for the allocation and management of the student assistant budget. Develops and implements new procedures, collects and analyzes user statistics regarding circulation, interlibrary loans, reserves, and makes recommendations regarding space utilization. Responsible for the interpretation and coordination of library policies and practices for Access Services. Responsible for collections in remote locations and for providing effective use of these collections. Coordinates the library's programs for both physical housing of collections and personal security. Works collaboratively with public and technical services departments to provide user-centered access services throughout the library system. Serves on the online systems team and also represents the University Libraries in local, regional, and national matters related to access services.

B. COLLECTION DEVELOPMENT

Collection Manager for Economics and International Documents. Responsible for all aspects of collection management and development of these collections, including selection of information resources; collection management, including storage, preservation, and weeding decisions; faculty liaison; collection interpretations, including specialized reference service and user instruction; collection evaluation; budgetary management, and resource sharing. Participates in the Social Sciences Collection Group.

C. LIBRARY AND PROFESSIONAL ACTIVITIES

Participates in professional activities, including service on library committees.

_____   _____
Signature of Employee   Date

_____   _____
Signature of Primary Supervisor/AUL   Date

The University of Chicago Library

Position Title: Assistant Director, Access & Facilities

Classification: Librarian, Level IV

Division: Access & Facilities Services

Summary Statement of Responsibilities:
Reporting to the Director of the University Library, this position is responsible for developing programs and services that provide and promote physical access to the general collections of the Joseph Regenstein Library. The position also takes a leadership role in coordinating access services with other divisions and other libraries within the University Library system. Access services includes circulation services; reserves processing; identification and privileges; entry control; interlibrary loan and document delivery; stacks maintenance and search services; current periodicals and microforms.

In addition, this position is responsible for facilities management, building services and shipping and receiving for the library system.

The Assistant Director, Access & Facilities, serves on University management bodies including the Administrative Committee, Library Council, standing committees and work group appointed to develop Library-wide plans, policies, programs, services and procedures.

The Assistant Director, Access & Facilities, also serves as a leader, mentor and facilitator for staff in the Division and advances the mission, vision, values and strategic plan of the Library through the work of the Division.

Representative Responsibilities:
- leads and manages 4 supervisors (Library Facilities Manager; Head, Access Services; Head, Regenstein Bookstacks, and Manager, Regenstein Periodicals and Microforms Reading Room), who, in turn, plan and direct the work of exempt, clerical and student staff throughout the Division
- in coordination with these supervisors, and other staff within the Division, establishes and maintains goals, priorities and programs for access services and facilities that are consistent with the University Library's mission and strategic plan
- serves as the primary contact and communicator for access services and policies for the University Library
- works closely with the Library Director and Administrative Manager to develop capital project requests for the Library system.
- communicates goals for Division/Library to staff, to the Library as a whole, and to other forums.
- communicates policies and divisional guidelines, plans and procedures to staff.
- brings potential problems to the attention of the Library Director or to other Administrative Committee members
- compiles regular and special reports; reviews operations and makes recommendations for improvements in service to users and working conditions for staff; estimates needs in terms of staff, equipment, etc., and provides justification.

June 30, 2004
Page 1

- conducts special studies as required; sets up and exercises quality and quantity controls for the division
- participates in Library management bodies, including the Administrative Committee; the Library Council and the Library Computing Council.
- effectively leads the monthly Access Committee and co-chairs the monthly Floor Coordinators meeting
- provides written reports, statistics, and proposals related to access services & facilities for the Library, University and other appropriate audiences
- represents the Library in local, regional and national forums related to access & facilities

Qualifications:
- Graduate degree in librarianship from a program accredited by the American Library Association
- Progressively responsible experience in academic research libraries
- Understanding of the broad issues facing research libraries, along with a good knowledge of librarianship
- Comprehensive knowledge of academic research libraries' processes and procedures, particularly those in the area of access and facilities services
- Significant supervisory and management experience
- Ability to relate to students, faculty and staff with sensitivity and to be responsive to the needs and concerns of the University and other library units
- Effective leadership in the development and implementation of new programs
- Ability to be creative in planning and knowledgeable about changing patterns of library operations
- Thorough understanding of national issues and developments in areas of access services and facilities
- Familiarity with trends in scholarly communication and research libraries
- Knowledge of the applications of information technology in access services and facilities management
- Strong customer service orientation
- Strong conceptual and analytical skills; excellent organizational skills
- Excellent written, oral and negotiating skills required

June 30, 2004
Page 2

The University of Connecticut Libraries

Job Description

Area:	**Access Services**
Title:	**Director of Library Access Services (Area Head)**
Salary Group:	**UCP XI**

Job Summary

Under the general direction of the Director of University Libraries, the Area Head administers, coordinates, and provides leadership in policy and program development for the Libraries' Access Services Area. The Area is comprised of Circulation/Reserves, including a General Information function, Document Delivery/Interlibrary Loan, and Culpeper Media Library Services. The incumbent also provides general leadership and coordination for access services operations at all University of Connecticut Libraries. Three University Librarians, fourteen University Library Assistant professional staff, and approximately twenty FTE student workers staff Access Services. The Area Head is a leader, mentor, and facilitator for staff in their operational service teams and advances the mission, vision, and strategic initiatives of the University Libraries through the work of the Area.

Together with five other Area Heads and the Director of University Libraries, the Area Head is a member of Leadership Council, the principal decision making body of the University Libraries. Within that context, the Area Head shares responsibility for the welfare of the University Libraries as a whole, including: participation in system-wide administrative processes; strategic planning; budgeting; personnel; resource allocation; and formulation of priorities, goals, policies and procedures.

Duties and Responsibilities

Planning and Organization

1. In coordination with Area staff, establishes and maintains Area goals, priorities, and programs consistent with the University Libraries' mission and strategic initiatives.
2. Administers and oversees area policies, processes, resource allocation, and evaluation of services in support of a team-based and client-centered Area environment.
3. Oversees Area workflow, based on a thorough knowledge of the technical systems supporting service goals and changing client needs.
4. Explores and applies developments in emerging information access technologies to advance client-centered, client-initiated services.
5. In conjunction with appropriate Library and University staff, participates in development activities that support their Areas.
6. Reviews Area needs for staff, space, equipment, and operating expenses.
7. Prepares Area budget requests and allocates and oversees management of budgets assigned to the Area.
8. Ensures that all required Area files and records are maintained in good order.

Personnel

1. Supervises the Circulation/Reserve Team Leader, the Document Delivery/Interlibrary Loan staff, and the Culpeper Media Library staff, including hiring, training, goals, and annual evaluations.
2. Makes recommendations for promotion, reclassification, merit increments, salary adjustments, and termination.
3. Prepares and ensures currency of job descriptions for all Area staff.
4. Proposes specific staffing needs and recruits new staff in a timely fashion when positions are approved. Recruits and retains minority staff members.
5. In coordination with area staff, plans training for new staff.
6. Practices conflict resolution and individual counseling in problematic situations for the Area's operational teams.
7. Serves as a mentor for Area staff and a facilitator for team-based activity within the Area. Creates an environment for Area staff that nurtures shared vision, diversity, and creativity. Models behavior desired in Area staff.
8. Initiates and charges specific project teams. Encourages and ensures team participation by necessary staff from outside of the Area.
9. Ensures that Area staff have skills and expertise commensurate to the rapidly changing technology for which they are responsible. Anticipates upcoming skills required and identifies specific training, development and education programs that meet those requirements.
10. Maintains a good working knowledge of library personnel policies, union contracts, and university policies to ensure that Area personnel procedures are in compliance.

Coordination/Communication

1. Ensures a regular flow of information and a forum for consensus decision-making through scheduled Area meetings and other appropriate means.
2. Serves as the primary contact and communicator for coordination of access services policies and procedures for Storrs Campus and all Regional Campus Libraries.
3. Serves as the Leadership Council liaison to appropriate Cross-Functional Teams and participates in appropriate Cross-Functional Teams.
4. Serves as the Area's liaison to University departments supporting the work of the Area: University Information Technology Services, Registrar's Office, Bursar's Office, Human Resources, Extended & Continuing Education, Graduate Records, One Card Office, Health Center and Law School Libraries.
5. Participates in weekly Leadership Council meetings, striving to achieve open communications and synergistic decision-making with colleagues.
6. Initiates communication with library clients as the work of the Area affects their use of the libraries.
7. Works with other libraries in the system and beyond to improve sharing and delivery of information in all formats.
8. Provides written reports, statistics, and proposals related to specific Area activities for Library, University, and other appropriate audiences.
9. Represents the University Libraries in local, regional, and national forums related to access services issues.

10. Maintains communication with vendors supporting the work of the area.

Functional Responsibilities

1. Oversees implementation and management of the Libraries' Access Services system projects. Leads teams assembled from various library and campus Areas and guides projects from concept to completion, including formally articulated library-wide goals.
2. Participates in the development, testing and documentation of projects and coordinates their transition to production.
3. Oversees client and staff user support, including: training, documentation, public programs, and user assistance.

Professional Development

1. Demonstrates commitment to structured continuous learning and motivates staff to engage in professional development activities.
2. Participates in continuing education in areas of expertise and responsibility and in management/leadership skills.
3. Maintains an awareness of University trends and trends in academic libraries related to resource sharing and the delivery of information.
4. Participates in appropriate professional activities at the local, regional, and national level, making significant professional contributions to advance the field.

Qualifications
Required

1. MLS from an ALA-accredited institution and at least 5 years of library managerial/supervisory, organizational, and leadership experience.
2. Demonstrated knowledge and experience with current and emerging trends and technologies related to circulation, electronic reserve, course management software, document delivery/interlibrary loan, multi-media, collection security, and collection storage and retrieval.
3. Experience with copyright law compliance issues, licensing in the networked environment, and privacy issues.
4. Ability to understand and creatively apply technology to a wide range of access services applications.
5. Ability to translate needs assessment into services.
6. Commitment to customer service and the ability to establish and maintain effective relationships with all library clientele.
7. Demonstrated commitment to consultation and cooperation with Library and University staff and users.
8. Demonstrated ability to work successfully in a rapidly changing environment and in group settings that facilitate discussion and build consensus.
9. Excellent organizational, interpersonal, oral and written communication skills.

Desired

1. Second appropriate graduate degree.
2. Experience in an academic library consortium environment.
3. Experience with the Endeavor Voyager and ENCompass products.
4. Experience in public relations work.
5. Record of relevant professional publications and activities.

The Gelman Library
CIRCULATION RESERVE DEPARTMENT
(revised July 1995)

DEPARTMENT / UNIT   : Circulation Services Department

JOB CLASSIFICATION   : LIBRARY MANAGER III (Grade 16)

FUNCTIONAL JOB TITLE   : Head, Circulation/Reserves Department

BASIC FUNCTION:
A position in which the incumbent reports to the Assistant University Librarian for Information Services, and supervises 3 service units with a staff of 9 full-time, 4 permanent part-time and 40-50 wage hour support staff in discharging the following responsibilities:

CHARACTERISTIC DUTIES AND RESPONSIBILITIES:

1. Overall responsibility for the supervision of the circulation and reserve service desks which circulate approximately 600,000 pieces of material yearly (including renewals) and collects approximately $80,000 annually in fines; for the supervision of the consortium loan service which borrows and lends approximately 18,000 items every year; and for the supervision of the reserve production unit which processes and maintains a reserve collection of 12,000 materials.

2. Administers a wage budget for the three units in the department and apprises unit coordinators of budget status through periodic reports; manages and controls expenditures with in the department.

3. Advises faculty, students, staff and other users on policy and procedures for utilization of library borrowing privileges; authorizes issuance of library cards to non-GWU users; interprets policy; and resolves problems and complaints.

4. Plans the overall operational direction of the department's goals by working with and through unit supervisors; directly coordinates and reviews the functional responsibilities of the department's administrative support staff and circulation control systems.

5. Consults with librarians and university officials from such offices as the Office of the Registrar, Student Accounts, chairs of the academic departments, faculty and teaching staff regarding circulation facilities, course reserve materials, study room assignments and allocations, encumbrances and bills, and advises them of possible implementation of new or improved methods.

6. Assists the administration of the library in development and maintenance of an online integrated library system which features a circulation/reserve system.

7. Assumes responsibility for the processing every semester of approximately 300-350 applications, and assignment of faculty and graduate students to 90 closed study rooms and 100 lockmobiles; resolves problems and complaints relating to closed study room use; and administers the physical and maintenance requirements (i.e. keys, light fixtures, housekeeping) to ensure that these study rooms are properly utilized.

8. Participates in library-wide policy making through membership in Programs and Services Group (PSG), Staff Management Group and other committees.

9. Prepares monthly statistical and narrative report; prepares other reports as requested, e.g. use of collections, requirements of user community.

10. Prepares staff performance evaluations and recommends to Assistant University Librarian for Information Services any changes in departmental policies and procedures regarding staff salaries and classifications.

11. Identifies training needs and works with Library and University officials to provide appropriate training.

12. Represents the Library in the WRLC Access Services Advisory Committee and consults with other circulation department heads regarding direct-borrowing policies and procedures.

SUPERVISION RECEIVED:

General supervision received weekly to monthly from the Assistant University Librarian for Information Services.

SUPERVISION EXERCISED:

Functional supervision is exercised directly over the three unit supervisors.
Overall supervision is exercised over 9 full-time and 3 permanent part-time staff and 40-50 wage hour support staff.

ENTRY LEVEL QUALIFICATIONS:

1. A bachelor's degree or an equivalent combination of training and experience is required.
2. Three to five years of progressively responsible library experience including one to two years of supervisory experience, is required.
3. Some graduate level work in library science is desirable.
4. Some knowledge of data processing input, output, and reporting potentials is desirable.
5. Excellent verbal and written English language communication skills are required.

Head, Access and Delivery Services

Position Description
Under the general direction of the Associate Director for Public Services, has responsibility for developing and managing an integrated service environment for the functions of circulation, bookstack maintenance, course reserves, current periodicals access, interlibrary loan/document delivery, microforms, laptop computer lending, and audiovisual service. Recommends, communicates, and administers fair, efficient circulation and access policies for the main library and four branches. Responsible for policy formulation and coordination of circulation/reserve functions in the library's integrated online system. Leads the library in defining and creating an innovative Multimedia Services Initiative, which will provide space, equipment, and staff to assist patrons in using the growing range of multimedia, full-text/image, and other non-print materials. Works cooperatively with the library's facilities manager and with the campus public safety office to ensure a safe and secure environment for users and staff. Works closely with branch librarians at NC State and with colleagues in the region and the state to improve responsiveness of circulation and interlibrary lending services. Develops departmental goals and objectives, prepares budget requests, manages budget allocations, and participates actively in library-wide planning processes. Serves as a member of the Libraries' Management Council and Public Services Heads group. Is active professionally.

Qualifications
Required: ALA-accredited MLS and 5 years relevant professional experience; or equivalent combination of education and experience. Experience in circulation and/or interlibrary loan operations and in management/supervision. Demonstrated commitment to providing highly responsive public service. Understanding of the mission of a research university and of the changing educational environment. Excellent interpersonal skills; ability to communicate clearly, knowledgeably, and personably, orally and in writing. Evidence of effective collaboration with faculty and students. Ability to lead and excel in a team environment. Demonstrated record of ongoing professional development.

Preferred: Demonstrated ability to design and implement innovative programs and services that advance organizational goals.

Position available immediately. Applications accepted until position is filled. Send cover letter (including title of position), resume, and the names, addresses, and telephone numbers of four current, professional references to: Wendy L. Scott, Office of Personnel Services; Box 7111, NCSU Libraries; Raleigh, NC 27695-7111

North Carolina State University is dedicated to equality of opportunity within its community.

THE UNIVERSITY OF OKLAHOMA
Library Faculty Vacancy

POSITION: HEAD, ACCESS SERVICES

DUTIES: Under the general direction of the Director of Information Management and Delivery, the Access Services Department Head is responsible for the following service areas: stack management, circulation, reserve, storage, interlibrary loan, document delivery and building security. The Access Services department is responsible for providing library users, local and remote, with physical access to the general collection in the main library and access to materials not held in the University Library Collections. Responsibilities of the Department Head include: definition and articulation of the role, goals, needs and policies of Access Services; supervision, training, and evaluation of one librarian, eight staff and 17 FTE student workers; development and determination of priorities used in decision-making for budgetary matters such as equipment and staffing; liaison with branches concerning circulation functions and the automated system; collection and analysis of appropriate statistical data; miscellaneous duties as assigned by the Director. This position is governed by the University's policies requiring research or creative achievement and professional service as outlined by the Faculty Handbook at http://www.ou.edu/provost/pronew/content/fhbmenu.html

QUALIFICATIONS: Required: MLS from ALA accredited library school; four years professional experience preferably in access services; substantial supervisory experience; demonstrated management skills; ability to work effectively with faculty, students and library staff; experience with major bibliographic utilities and library system software; effective oral and written communication skills; evidence of research or creative achievement. Desirable: Second master's degree; experience with SIRSI, Unicorn system.

SEARCH WILL REMAIN OPEN UNTIL FILLED

SALARY: Commensurate with qualifications and experience.

BENEFITS: TIAA/CREF; State Retirement System; 33 days paid leave; University holidays; comprehensive medical protection; group life insurance; and reduced tuition.

UNIVERSITY LIBRARIES: A member of the Research Libraries Group, AMIGOS, and ARL, the University Libraries consists of a main library and six branches. The collection contains more than 4.1 million volumes, 16,000 periodical subscriptions, and three outstanding special collections in history of science, western history, and business history. The Libraries operates a computerized library system (SIRSI) for local holdings. The libraries provide access to document delivery via Uncover and access to electronic resources including FirstSearch, Searchbank/InfoTrac, Lexis/Nexis and JSTOR. The University of Oklahoma Libraries is a NACO contributing library. The Libraries' home page is http://www.ou.edu/libraries/ Norman, Oklahoma is an attractive community close to a major metropolitan city with a low cost of living.

EMPLOYMENT: Librarians have faculty status, privileges, responsibilities, rank of assistant professor or above, and are eligible for tenure.

APPLICATION: Send letter of application with resume, a list of publications and the names of three references including current supervisor to: Donald C. Hudson, Director of Administrative Services, University Libraries, University of Oklahoma, Norman, OK 73019, (405) 325-2611.

OKLAHOMA UNIVERSITY IS AN EQUAL OPPORTUNITY/AFFIRMATIVE ACTION EMPLOYER
WE ENCOURAGE WOMEN AND MINORITY APPLICANTS AND
WE ARE RESPONSIVE TO THE NEEDS OF DUAL CAREER COUPLES

Statement of Core Responsibilities

The Head of Access Services holds primary responsibility for leadership and oversight of the five units in the department: Lending Services, Collection Maintenance and Annex Operations, Interlibrary Loan, Academic Course Reserves, and Library Services for Persons with Disabilities. One of the largest departments in the University Libraries, Access Services includes 50 full-time and approximately 75 part-time staff members (22 FTE). Reporting to the Associate Dean for University Park Libraries, this position works closely with Public Services operations to ensure appropriate levels of access to library collections. The Head of Access Services collaborates with the Head of Public Services and the Associate Dean for Campus College Libraries in leading cross-unit initiatives in user services. To carry out this assignment, responsibilities include:

- Providing administrative oversight, including budget planning, establishing policies and procedures, and personnel management for the Department.
- Maintaining knowledge of current national developments and trends in all areas of access services.
- Fostering a commitment to the application of current and emerging technologies to enhance library services.
- Creating and maintaining a work environment that supports staff development and growth.
- Fostering communication across Libraries' departments and Penn State campuses.
- Engaging in assessment of services and programs to benchmark progress and effectiveness.
- Creating a climate that ensures an effective service-oriented philosophy throughout the organization.
- Providing leadership in the ongoing development of new and existing user services in all areas of the access services.
- Participating in the ongoing planning, maintenance, and development of the Libraries' online catalog and web-based services as they pertain to Access Services.
- Representing the Libraries in ongoing resource sharing and consortial relationships.

In addition, the Head of Access Services is expected to participate in activities related to library governance and library-wide efforts to develop systems and services, and to devote time to research, scholarly activity, and service to the University, the society, and the profession.

PRINCETON UNIVERSITY LIBRARY

HUMAN RESOURCES

Library Home   Library HR   Library Staff Directory   University HR   University Home

Positions

How to Apply for Library Jobs

Library Assistant Vacancies

Hourly Position Vacancies

Professional and Administrative Vacancies

Fellowships

Relocation Information

Student Employment

Training/Development

Support Staff Info

Forms/Procedures

Committees/Groups

Site Map

Circulation Services Director
Firestone Library
Princeton, New Jersey

The Princeton University Library, one of the world's most respected research institutions, serves a diverse community of 6,600 students and 1,100 faculty members with more than 6 million printed volumes, 5 million manuscripts, and 2 million non print items. The holdings in its central library and 15 specialized libraries range from ancient papyri and incunabula to the most advanced electronic databases and digital collections. The Library employs a dedicated and knowledgeable staff of more than 300 professional and support personnel, complemented by a large student and hourly workforce. More information can be found at the Library's Web site: http://libweb.princeton.edu

Available: Immediately

Search Committee: (Princeton Access Only)

Description: Princeton University Library seeks an innovative service-oriented manager to lead its Circulation Division. The Circulation Division is comprised of 4 professional staff, 28 support staff and 70 student assistants and employs the Voyager integrated library management system for core circulation functions. The Circulation Services Director has overall responsibility for management of circulation, shelving, stack maintenance and related system record management, and space planning for collections totaling more than 3,000,000 volumes held by the main library and the Library's two storage annexes. This position is also responsible for providing overall direction of circulation policy for the Princeton University Library system, working closely with heads of branches and special collections to promote user services and access to the collections, to maximize efficient use of Voyager circulation functionality, and to increase the quantity and quality of management data to support planning for library circulation and space needs. The Circulation Services Director coordinates assessment of the library's long-range space requirements and the development of plans to meet them, and leads the planning and management team which is responsible for library-wide holdings transfers to remote storage. The Circulation Services Director directly supervises Reserve/General Periodicals Services, comprising the library's primary print and electronic course reserve service and a general periodicals collection of approximately 4,200 journals. The Circulation Services Director serves as one of the library's key liaisons to the university's Office of Information Technology in matters that relate to library circulation and reserve services, such as development of Blackboard courseware. This position works closely and collaboratively with subject specialists in collection development, branch library heads and technical processing managers on space planning, development of access services and Voyager circulation system issues, and has special responsibility for leadership in these areas. The Circulation Services Director must be a proactive leader in a dynamic, rapidly changing work environment focused on the continuous improvement and expansion of patron access services and must be dedicated to and capable of developing staff to support such services. It is expected that the Circulation Services Director will be active in national forums related to access services and library space planning. This position reports to the Associate University Librarian for Technical Services.

Qualifications: *Required:* MLS from an ALA accredited institution or equivalent combination of education and professional experience. A minimum of five years relevant professional experience in an academic or research library, or the equivalent, which must include a minimum of three years of supervisory and management experience on a scale and of a complexity sufficient to indicate the likelihood of success in the position being advertised. Relevant knowledge of and experience with library circulation systems, access services and supporting technology. Experience which demonstrates a strong service orientation and a commitment to staff development; strong interpersonal skills; strong team work and team building skills; strong planning, organization and problem-solving skills; strong oral and written communication skills; and well-developed computer skills.

Preferred: Knowledge of and experience with online library information services and data bases, and/or contemporary interlibrary loan and/or document delivery systems and services. Participation in relevant national forums. Experience with catalog maintenance functions or other relevant online record management.

Compensation and Benefits: Compensation will be competitive and commensurate with experience and accomplishments. Twenty-four (24) vacation days a year, plus eleven (11) paid holidays. Annuity program (TIAA/CREF), group life insurance, health coverage insurance, disability insurance, and other benefits are available.

Nominations and Applications: Review of applications will begin immediately and will continue until the position is filled. Nominations and applications (resume and the names, titles, addresses and phone numbers of three references) should be sent as an MSWord attachment via e-mail to libhrpro@princeton.edu or by fax to (609-258-0454).

Submissions via regular mail are also welcomed and can be sent to:

Search Committee for Circulation Services Director
c/o Lila Fredenburg, Human Resources Librarian
Princeton University Library
One Washington Road
Princeton, New Jersey 08544-2098

***PRINCETON UNIVERSITY IS AN EQUAL OPPORTUNITY / AFFIRMATIVE ACTION
EMPLOYER***

© 2003 Princeton University   Last Updated 09/28/2005   Content Manager Luisa Paster

Purdue University Libraries
March 2005

Head, Access Services
Position Description

Overall management and responsibility for the development, implementation, improvement, and evaluation of services, programs, policies, and practices within the four units that comprise Access Services. Write management reports and compile and interpret statistical data. Supervise unit heads, other professionals, and the clerical staff in the Storage Facility. Monitor budgets. Compile and interpret statistics. Write reports. Represent the Purdue University Libraries in consortial resource sharing groups and coordinate resource sharing services with consortial partners. Represent Access Services on the Libraries Management Team.

Responsible for these four units and their activities:

Interlibrary Loan. Borrowing and lending services. Campus document delivery services (books only, to faculty and staff). ILL book purchase program (Books on Demand).

Circulation Services. Pre-billing activities. File transfers to Accounts Receivable. Issue borrowing cards to visitors and reciprocal borrowers. System-wide circulation and reserves training.

Storage Facility. On-campus facility for lesser used library materials.

Technical Information Service (fee-based information service). Deliver information services and document delivery on a cost-recovery basis to the business community.

[draft]

**University of Utah
Marriott Library
Position Description**

Name: **Linda Burns**
Position: **Head of Circulation and Interlibrary Loans**
Department: **Public Services**
Date: **January, 2001**

General Description

The Head of Circulation and Interlibrary Loans, reporting to the Assistant Director for Public Services, oversees the planning, development, and provision of innovative, creative and proactive user-centered services of the Marriott Library Circulation Department. Selects, trains, supervises and evaluates staff. Works closely with other Public Services departments, and with Collection Development, Technical Services, Special Collections, and Library Computing.

Duties and Responsibilities

Responsible for the administration and leadership of the Circulation Department, including the library's main circulation desk, two exit desks, Stacks, and Interlibrary Loans.

Based on the goals and priorities of the library and the needs of users, applies creative leadership in the planning, development, provision, and evaluation of the library's Circulation programs and services, emphasizing the delivery of quality service to library users as the preeminent value and function; prepares short and long term goals for the department.

Works closely with Circulation staff, the Implementation Task Force, and others to determine the feasibility of the Access Services Task Force recommendations and to lead in planning and implementation.

Responsible for hiring, supervision and evaluation of staff in Circulation, Stacks and Interlibrary Loans.

Ensures that training is continuous and consistent for all staff.

Exemplifies a level of excellence in the provision of circulation services that serves as a model for Circulation staff and helps to set a service tone for the entire library.

Ensures accurate and timely handling of circulated materials through error free check-in and check-out procedures.

Keeps users up-to-date about due dates and recall notifications through the timely issuance of circulation statements.

Promotes careful and professional arbitration of user conflicts that allow for teaching users about policies, not overly punishing them, yet instilling a sense of user responsibility for their use of library materials; resolves patron conflicts referred from other staff.

Ensures proper maintenance of library collections in precise call number order through accurate and timely reshelving of materials and regular shelf reading done by Stacks staff.

Provides for the borrowing and lending of library resources through an effective Interlibrary Loans section. Continues to contribute some time to ILL processing of requests from users and libraries.

Integrates new information technology and electronic formats with Circulation and Interlibrary Loans services and operations by being knowledgeable of developments and trends in the storage, retrieval and delivery of information resources; directs enhancements of the automated circulation subsystem.

Manages Circulation budgets, planning resources for the short and long term benefit of services.

Supports the library's growing teaching program by fostering an environment where Circulation staff help users learn about library services and policies; fosters participation of Circulation staff in instruction activities as appropriate.

Coordinates with the Collection Development Department to provide Circulation Department data on collection management and patron use of materials.

Works closely with other Public Services and library departments to plan and coordinate service programs in a library-wide environment focused on users.

Participates in the management of the library through membership on the Marriott Advisory Council and relevant committees and task forces.

Participates in library-wide planning process.

Performs other duties as appropriate.

P112-PD (rev 1/03)

 Virginia Polytechnic Institute and State University
EMPLOYEE WORK PROFILE P112

SECTION ONE: POSITION DESCRIPTION
Used to establish new positions, fill existing positions, and make role changes

PART I: REASON FOR SUBMISSION (check appropriate blocks):

☐ Request to Fill Vacancy   ☐ New Position   ☒ Job Description Update
☐ Role Change*   ☐ Change % Time (e.g. P/T to F/T)
*Requested Role Title: _____   Date Prepared: _____

PART II: RECRUITMENT INFORMATION:

Department Contact: _____   Phone Number: _____
E-Mail Address: _____   Fax Number: _____
Recruitment Type: ☐ Open to employees and general public
     ☐ Restricted to employees only   Date to Fill Vacancy: _____

PART III: POSITION IDENTIFICATION INFORMATION

Position Number: 007817	Department Name: University Libraries
Current or Last Incumbent:	Department Number: 0241
Role Title: Library Specialist II	Work Location (for off-campus only):
Work Title: Unite Head, Circulation/Reserve/Storage	Hours Per Week: 40	Work Schedule: M-F, 8-5 and as needed to carry out unit head duties
Pay Band: 4	Type of Appointment: ☒ CY Salary ☐ AY Salary ☐ Wage
Supervisor's Name: Donald J. Kenney	Renewed Yearly: (for sponsored accounts only) ☐ Yes ☐ No
Supervisor's Title Associate Dean of Administrative Services	End Date (If restricted or AY):
Supervisor's Position Number: FA176	Funding (% for each): 121315 100%

Personnel Services use only:

ROLE CODE: _____   SOC CODE: _____   FLSA Status: ☐ Exempt ☐ Non-Exempt

Job Group _____   EEO Category _____   Date Effective: _____

Level: ☐ Employee ☐ Supervisor ☐ Manager   Approved By: _____

PART IV: JOB SUMMARY AND QUALIFICATIONS

Chief Objective of Position: To manage and provide leadership to ensure prompt, courteous, and accurate service provided by the Circulation Desk, the Document Delivery Service, and the storage facility; to facilitate the security of Newman Library; to problem solve creatively to meet the needs of a changing academic library environment and to work cooperatively in a team spirit with other units throughout the library system; to nurture staff to manage their jobs in a flexible, changing environment.

Qualifications:
- Ability to independently resolve problems; deal with a variety of publics; possess good organizational and managerial skills; ability to work without close supervision and independently make decisions; ability to plan and execute projects
- Broad based computer skills: word processing, spreadsheets, and some graphic skills; familiarity and ability to use the internet

- Experience working with the public and in particular a highly public visible environment; ability to work with other library units in a collaborative/cooperative environment
- Ability to coordinate the work of staff performing tasks in multiple buildings and working with a variety of schedules; prioritize and organize work tasks with attention to detail; adaptable to changes in workflow and procedures and fluctuating workloads
- Ability to interpret, to explain, and to apply library policies to the public
- Knowledge of research library practices and procedures; a minimum of 5 years of academic library experience preferred
- Knowledge of library OPAC systems with preference given for familiarity with VTLS operations and software applications
- Ability to maintain a professional manner in emotional and confrontational situations;
- Strong oral and written communication skills
- Flexibility in dealing with deadlines and unpredictable office workflow

Preferences: College degree preferred and/or experience in an academic library working with the public and with supervisory/managerial experience in an academic library environment
-

Education, Licensure, Certification required for entry into position:
Bachelor's degree preferred and/or training in secretarial, administrative or business related field

---

Does the employee supervise 2 or more Full Time Equivalent employees: ☒ Yes ☐ No

Which of the following are required to meet legal and policy requirements?

☐ Commercial Driver's License (CDL)	☐ Criminal History check	☒ Driver's license
☐ Drug screening	☐ Medical exam	☐ Other, specify:

PART V: PHYSICAL REQUIREMENTS

Check the physical activities required to perform the **essential** functions of the position:

☒	Light lifting (<20 lbs.)	☒	Standing	☒	Sitting	☒	Bending
☐	Moderate lifting (20-50 lbs.)	☒	Lifting	☒	Walking	☒	Climbing
☐	Heavy lifting (>50 lbs.)	☒	Reaching	☒	Repetitive motion	☒	Pushing/pulling
☐	Other, specify:						

PART VI: CORE RESPONSIBILITIES

%	Describe major responsibilities in each functional area of responsibility.
50%	. Manages the daily operations of the Circulation/Reserve, document delivery service in the main library, the operations of the library remote storage facility (approx. 14 FTE) and wage employees (including student assistants): • Plans, coordinates, and manages the work of each area: assesses workflow, assignments, and prioritizes job assignments. Ensures that there is adequate coverage in all areas of responsibility for all the operating hours. • Works with the Records Management Services Department manager on maintaining access to the storage facility, security procedures, and any operational decisions that have an impact on both the library and Records management Services. • Approves all vacation requests based on coverage and shifts schedules accordingly. • Develops, documents, and implements programs and procedures to improve the effectiveness and efficiency of unit operations. Establishes long term planning by setting unit goals and preparing student wage and supply budget requests. • Acts as library resource for circulation/reserve issues by consulting with branch libraries and interlibrary loan to ensure consistent administration of policies and procedures among university libraries, for other departments on campus, and for various group/organizations inquiring about library privileges. • Fosters team work and collaboration and uses data-based decision making and problem solving processes to effectively manage the unit.
30%	Manages the performance of subordinates in such a way that:

P112-PD (rev 1/03)

	• expectations are clear and well communicated and relate to the goals and objectives of the department and unit; • subordinates receive frequent feedback; • unit staff have the necessary knowledge, skills and abilities to accomplish unit goals; • the requirements of the performance planning and evaluation system are met and performance evaluations are completed by established deadline with proper documentation; • performance issues are addressed as they occur
10%	Serves as a contact person for campus security during all hours the main library and the storage facility are open: • Reports to campus security any emergencies, security violations, and disruptive behavior in the library. Whenever necessary, contacts campus security, as well as other library and/or university employees needed to assist with the situation. • Works with campus security to ensure that proper procedures are followed at opening and closing times (alarms turned off/on, entrance doors locked/unlocked, security logs kept up to date) informs campus security of any changes in operating hours so that security will be maintained in the building. Supervisors all in-house security employees (1 FTE and wage employees).
5%	• Serves as the reviewer for any appeals submitted by library patrons. As necessary, reviews decisions made by other circulation staff and makes independent decision that is documented. • Assists at the checkin counter; maintains a detailed knowledge of checkin and shelving procedures; ensures coordination and consistency between circulation and shelving. • Participates in demonstrating to visitors the University Libraries circulation functions and activities at the storage facility.
5%	• As a team member continuously collaborates with colleagues through good communications and listening skills and through active participation in order to achieve consensus in accomplishing goals. • Performs other duties as assigned. • Adapts easily and readily to changes in workflow, assignments, and office changes • Responds willingly to changes in procedures, technology, responsibility, or assignment

PART VII: APPROVALS

Supervisor's Name: Donald J. Kenney   FA176   Position Number   #Number   Signature: _____   Date: _____

Reviewer's Name: Eileen Hitchingham   FA082   Position Number   Signature: _____   Date: _____

Hiring Authority's Name: Donald J. Kenney   Position Number   Signature _____   Date: _____

Attach an organizational chart showing where position fits in organizational unit.

UNIVERSITY OF WASHINGTON

UNIVERSITY OF WASHINGTON LIBRARIES

<u>Office of the Director</u>

<u>POSITION DESCRIPTION</u>

April 30, 1991

NAME: Thomas Deardorff

POSITION TITLE: Coordinator for Access Services

GENERAL DESCRIPTION: The Coordinator for Access Services reports to the Associate Director of Libraries, Public Services and is responsible for providing overall management and policy guidance for the Circulation Division, Resources Sharing Service; Interlibrary Borrowing Service and campus-wide document delivery; developing and implementing programs for services and contributing to the management of public services and the Libraries. Coordinates the systemwide formulation and implementation of access policies in relation to circulation, resource sharing, interlibrary loan and document delivery.

SPECIFIC RESPONSIBILITIES: Facilitates understanding among Access Services staff of the current priorities and objectives of the University of Washington Libraries. Establishes policies, programs and services in accordance with these priorities and objectives, with approval of Associate Director of Libraries, Public Services.

Coordinates the activities of Access Services to maximize the accessibility of the collections for use by the Libraries' users, while maintaining concern for proper care and preservation of library material.

Recommends hiring and termination of unit professional staff. Supervises, develops and evaluates the Heads of the Circulation Division, the Resources Sharing Service and the Interlibrary Borrowing Service. Insures appropriate development opportunities for all staff.

Plans and implements a campus-wide document delivery service. Develops a pilot program as a part of long-range plan for campus document access.

Assess library users' access requirements and develop programs to respond to those needs.

Manages the implementation of automated circulation and participates in planning library automated systems.

Assumes other responsibilities as assigned; performs other duties as required.

WASHINGTON UNIVERSITY LIBRARIES

LIBRARY POSITION

POSITION TITLE: Head of Access

REPORTS TO: Assistant Dean for Access, Bibliographic, and Information Services

SUMMARY: The Head of Access is responsible for providing flexible, responsive leadership in the management of the Reserve, Circulation, Interlibrary Loan, Shelving, and Arc: Technology Center units, developing and coordinating access policies and procedures among Olin and the departmental and school libraries, and managing the Library's participation in consortial resource sharing programs. Serves as a member of the Library Administrative Group.

QUALIFICATIIONS:

Education

> MLS from an ALA accredited library school.
> Second master's degree preferred.

Experience

> At least three years of supervisory experience, preferably in an academic library.
> Experience with the operation of an automated library management system.
> Strong customer service orientation.
> Excellent communication skills.
> Ability to work effectively in a collegial manner in a changing environment.
> Understanding of the information needs of a research university.
> Experience in academic library circulation, reserve, or ILL/document delivery services preferred.
> Experience with providing access to multi-media resources preferred.

DUTIES:

Develop and manage a program of user-centered access services.	30%
Ensure the efficient and effective operation of the Reserve, Circulation, Interlibrary Loan, Shelving, and Arc: Technology Center units.	25%
Coordinate the Library's participation in customer-initiated document delivery services and consortial resource sharing.	15%
Interview, select, supervise, evaluate and make recommendations regarding personnel in the Audio-Visual/Reserve, Circulation, Interlibrary Loan, and Shelving Units.	10%
Coordinate access policies and procedures among Olin and the departmental libraries.	10%
Work cooperatively with the Library's Director of Administration and Planning and with appropriate campus officials to ensure a safe and secure environment for users and collections.	5%
Ensure the implementation of University and Library policies.	5%

SELECTED RESOURCES

DOCUMENTS

Journal Articles

Austin, Brice, Tim Byrne, Ann Miller, Michael Riberdy, and Curt Williams. "Procedures to Follow If a Law Enforcement Official Asks for Patron Information: A Checklist for Access Services Student Employees." *Journal of Access Services* 2, no. 2 (2004): 1–22.

Gohlke, Mary Jo, and Kathlin Ray. "Impacts of an Information Commons on an Academic Library's Service Points." *Journal of Access Services* 1, no. 3 (2003): 57–72.

Hasty, Douglas F. "Applying Fourth Generation Management to Access Services: Reinventing Customer Service and Process Management." *Journal of Access Services* 2, no. 3 (2004): 21–42.

Hersey, Denise P. "The Future of Access Services: Should There Be One?" *Journal of Access Services* 2, no. 4 (2004): 1–6.

Lee, Leslie A., and Michelle M. Wu. "Personnel Management in Access Services: A General Overview of the Literature, 1990–2002" *Journal of Access Services* 1, no. 4 (2003): 5–44.

Sapp, Gregg. "On Access Services Recruiting Future Library Leaders." *Journal of Access Services* 1, no. 3 (2003): 1–4.

Tolppanen, Bradley P. "A Survey of Current Tasks and Future Trends in Access Services." *Journal of Access Services* 2, no. 3 (2004): 1–20.

Additional Circulation/Access Services Web Sites

Case Western Reserve University
http://library.case.edu/ksl/services/circ/

Colorado State University
http://lib.colostate.edu/access/

University of Connecticut
> http://www.lib.uconn.edu/about/services/circulation/

Florida State University
> http://www.lib.fsu.edu/circulation/circulation.html

University of Hawaii at Manoa
> http://libweb.hawaii.edu/libdept/access/access.htm

University of Illinois at Chicago
> http://www.uic.edu/depts/lib/circulation/

Kent State University
> http://www.library.kent.edu/page/10266

University of Louisville
> http://library.louisville.edu/ekstrom/circulation/circ/

University of Missouri
> http://mulibraries.missouri.edu/AccessServices/circ.html

Northwestern University
> http://www.library.northwestern.edu/circulation/index.html

Pennsylvania State University
> http://www.libraries.psu.edu/tas/lending/

Virginia Tech
> http://www.lib.vt.edu/services/circ-reserve/

Library Services Web Sites

Boston College
> http://www.bc.edu/libraries/services/

University of California, Irvine
> http://www.lib.uci.edu/services/services.html

University of California, San Diego
> http://sshl.ucsd.edu/services/index.html

George Washington University
> http://www.gwu.edu/gelman/services.html

University of Wisconsin–Madison
> http://www.library.wisc.edu/services/

Yale University
> http://www.library.yale.edu/services/

Note: All URLs accessed October 24, 2005.

SPEC KIT TITLE LIST

SP290   Access Services
SP289   Managing Large Projects
SP288   Scanning Services for Library Users
SP287   Instructional Improvement Programs
SP286   Collab for Dist Learn Info Lit Instr
SP285   Lib Svcs in Non-Library Spaces
SP284   Security in Special Collections
SP283   Grant Coordination
SP282   Managing Electronic Resources
SP281   The Information Commons
SP280   Library User Surveys
SP279   Evaluating Library Instruction
SP278   Library Patron Privacy
SP277   Lib Pub Acc Workstation Auth
SP276   Recruitment and Retention
SP275   Laptop Computer Services
SP274   Data Mining & Warehousing
SP273   Chat Reference
SP272   Insuring & Valuing Res Lib Coll
SP271   Lib Systems Office Organization
SP270   Core Competencies
SP269   Integrating Preserv Activities
SP268   Reference Statistics
SP267   User Authentication
SP266   Staffing the Library Website
SP265   Instructional Support Services
SP264   Extended Library Hours
SP263   Numeric Data Services
SP262   Preservation & Digitization
SP261   Post-Tenure Review
SP260   Interview Process
SP259   Fee-based Services
SP258   Corporate Annual Reports
SP257   MLS Hiring Requirement
SP256   Changing Roles of Lib Profs
SP255   Branch Libs/Discrete Collectns
SP254   Managing Printing Services
SP253   Networked Info Services
SP252   Supprt Staff Classifictn Studies
SP251   Electronic Reference Service
SP250   TL10: Educating Faculty
SP249   Catalogng of Resrces Digitized
SP248   Licensing of Electronic Prodcts
SP247   Management of Lib Security
SP246   Web Page Devel & Managmnt
SP245   Electronic Reserves Operations
SP244   TL 9: Renovation & Reconfigur
SP243   TL 8: Users with Disabilities
SP242   Library Storage Facilities
SP241   Gifts and Exchange Function
SP240   Marketing and PR Activities
SP239   Mentoring Programs in ARL
SP238   ARL GIS Literacy Project
SP237   Managing Food and Drink
SP236   TL 7: E-Theses/Dissertations
SP235   Collaborative Coll Management

SP234   TL 6: Distance Learning
SP233   ARL in Extension/Outreach
SP232   Use of Teams in ARL
SP231   Cust Service Programs in ARL
SP230   Affirmative Action in ARL
SP229   Evaluating Acad Libr Dirs
SP228   TL 5: Preserving Digital Info
SP227   Org of Doc Coll & Svcs
SP226   TL 4: After the User Survey
SP225   Partnerships Program
SP224   Staff Training & Development
SP223   TL 3: Electronic Scholarly Pubn
SP222   Electronic Resource Sharing
SP221   Evol & Status of Approval Plans
SP220   Internet Training
SP219   TL 2: Geographic Info Systems
SP218   Info Technology Policies
SP217   TL 1: Electronic Reserves
SP216   Role of Libs in Distance Ed
SP215   Reorg & Restructuring
SP214   Digit Tech for Preservation
SP213   Tech Svcs Workstations
SP212   Non-Librarian Professionals
SP211   Library Systems Office Org
SP210   Strategic Planning
SP209   Library Photocopy Operations
SP208   Effective Library Signage
SP207   Org of Collection Develop
SP206   Faculty Organizations
SP205   User Surveys in ARL Libs
SP204   Uses of Doc Delivery Svcs
SP203   Reference Svc Policies
SP202   E-journals/Issues & Trends
SP201   E-journals/Pol & Proced
SP200   2001: A Space Reality
SP199   Video Collect & Multimedia
SP198   Automating Preserv Mgt
SP197   Benefits/Professional Staff
SP196   Quality Improve Programs
SP195   Co-op Strategies in Foreign Acqs
SP194   Librarian Job Descriptions
SP193   Lib Develop & Fundraising
SP192   Unpub Matls/Libs, Fair Use
SP191   Prov Pub Svcs Remote User
SP190   Chang Role of Book Repair
SP189   Liaison Svcs in ARL Libs
SP188   Intern, Residency & Fellow
SP187   ILL Trends/Staff & Organ
SP186   Virtual Library
SP185   System Migration
SP184   ILL Trends/Access
SP183   Provision of Comp Print Cap
SP182   Academic Status for Libns
SP181   Perf Appr of Collect Dev Libn
SP180   Flexible Work Arrangemts
SP179   Access Services Org & Mgt
SP178   Insuring Lib Colls & Bldgs
SP177   Salary Setting Policies
SP176   Svcs for Persons w/Disabilities

SP175   Scholarly Info Centrs
SP174   Expert Systems
SP173   Staff Recognition Awards
SP172   Information Desks
SP171   Training of Tech Svc Staff
SP170   Organization Charts
SP169   Mgt of CD-ROM
SP168   Student Employment
SP167   Minority Recruitment
SP166   Materials Budgets
SP165   Cultural Diversity
SP164   Remote Storage
SP163   Affirmative Action
SP162   Audiovisual Policies
SP161   Travel Policies
SP160   Preservation Org & Staff
SP159   Admin of Lib Computer Files
SP158   Strategic Plans
SP157   Fee-based Services
SP156   Automating Authority Control
SP155   Visiting Scholars/Access
SP154   Online Biblio Search
SP153   Use of Mgt Statistics
SP152   Brittle Books Program
SP151   Qualitative Collect Analysis
SP150   Bldg Security & Personal Safety
SP149   Electronic Mail
SP148   User Surveys
SP147   Serials Control/Deselection
SP146   Lib Dev Fund Raising Capabilit
SP145   Lib Publications Programs
SP144   Building Use Policies
SP143   Search Proced Sr LibAdmin
SP142   Remote Access Online Cats
SP141   Approval Plans
SP140   Performance Appraisal
SP139   Performance Eval: Ref Svcs
SP138   University Copyright
SP137   Preservation Guidelines
SP136   Managing Copy Cataloging
SP135   Job Analysis
SP134   Planning Mgt Statistics
SP133   Opt Disks: Storage & Access
SP132   Library-Scholar Communication
SP131   Coll Dev Organization
SP130   Retrospective Conversion
SP129   Organization Charts
SP128   Systems File Organization
SP127   Interlibrary Loan
SP126   Automated Lib Systems
SP125   Tech Svcs Cost Studies
SP124   Barcoding of Collections
SP123   Microcomp Software Policies
SP122   End-User Search Svcs
SP121   Bibliographic Instruction
SP120   Exhibits
SP119   Catalog Maintenance Online
SP118   Unionization
SP117   Gifts & Exchange Function

SP116 Organizing for Preservation
SP115 Photocopy Services
SP114 Binding Operations
SP113 Preservation Education
SP112 Reorg of Tech and Pub Svcs
SP111 Cooperative Collection Dev
SP110 Local Cataloging Policies
SP109 Staff Training for Automation
SP108 Strategic Planning
SP107 University Archives
SP106 Electronic Mail
SP105 Nonbibliographic Dbases
SP104 Microcomputers
SP103 Asst/Assoc Dir Position
SP102 Copyright Policies
SP101 User Studies
SP100 Collection Security
SP099 Branch Libraries
SP098 Telecommunications
SP097 Building Renovation
SP096 Online Catalogs
SP095 Lib Materials Cost Studies
SP094 Fund Raising
SP093 User Instructions for Online Cats
SP092 Interlibrary Loan
SP091 Student Assistants
SP090 Integrated Lib Info Systems
SP089 Tech Svcs Cost Studies
SP088 Corporate Use of Research Libs
SP087 Collect Descript/Assessment
SP086 Professional Development
SP085 Personnel Classification Sys
SP084 Public Svcs Goals & Objectvs
SP083 Approval Plans
SP082 Document Delivery Systems
SP081 Services to the Disabled
SP080 Specialty Positions
SP079 Internships/Job Exchanges
SP078 Recruitment-Selection

SP077 Use of Small Computers
SP076 Online Biblio Search Svcs
SP075 Staff Development
SP074 Fees for Services
SP073 External User Services
SP072 Executive Review
SP071 User Surveys: Eval of Lib Svcs
SP070 Preservation Procedures
SP069 Prep Emergencies/Disasters
SP068 AACR2 Implement Studies
SP067 Affirm Action Programs
SP066 Planning Preserv of Lib Mat
SP065 Retrospective Conversion
SP064 Indirect Cost Rates
SP063 Collective Bargaining
SP062 Online Biblio Search Svcs
SP061 Status of Librarians
SP060 Lib Materials Cost Studies
SP059 Microform Collections
SP058 Goals & Objectives
SP057 Special Collections
SP056 External Communication
SP055 Internl Com/Staff & Super Role
SP054 Internal Com/Policies & Proced
SP053 Performance Appraisal
SP052 Cost Studies & Fiscal Plan
SP051 Professional Development
SP050 Fringe Benefits
SP049 Use of Annual Reports
SP048 External Fund Raising
SP047 Automated Cataloging
SP046 Plan Future of Card Catalog
SP045 Changing Role Personnel Officer
SP044 Automated Acquisitions
SP043 Automated Circulation Sys
SP042 Resource Sharing
SP041 Collection Assessment
SP040 Skills Training
SP039 Remote Storage

SP038 Collection Dev Policies
SP037 Theft Detection & Prevent
SP036 Allocation Materials Funds
SP035 Preservation of Lib Materials
SP034 Determin Indirect Cost Rate
SP033 Intergrat Nonprint Media
SP032 Prep, Present Lib Budget
SP031 Allocation of Resources
SP030 Support Staff, Student Assts
SP029 Systems Function
SP028 Gifts & Exchange Function
SP027 Physical Access
SP026 Bibliographic Access
SP025 User Statistics and Studies
SP024 User Surveys
SP023 Grievance Policies
SP022 Private Foundations
SP021 Paraprofessionals
SP020 Managerial Technical Specialists
SP019 Staff Allocations
SP018 Staff Development
SP017 Library Instruction
SP016 Reclassification
SP015 Goals & Objectives
SP014 Performance Review
SP013 Planning Systems
SP012 Acquisition Policies
SP011 Collection Development
SP010 Leave Policies
SP009 Tenure Policies
SP008 Collective Bargaining
SP007 Personnel Class Schemes
SP006 Friends of the Lib Organization
SP005 Performance Review
SP004 Affirmative Action
SP003 A Personnel Organization
SP003 Status of Librarians
SP002 Personnel Survey (flyer only)
SP001 Organization Charts

SPEC Kit Price Information (ISSN 0160 3582)

Subscription (6 issues per year; shipping included): $205 ARL members/$275 nonmembers (Additional postage may apply outside North America.)

Individual Kits: $35 ARL members/$45 nonmembers, plus shipping and handling.

Individual issues of the Transforming Libraries (TL) subseries: $28, plus shipping and handling.

Shipping & Handling

U.S.: UPS Ground delivery, $10 per publication.

Canada: UPS Ground delivery, $15 per publication

International and rush orders: Call or e-mail for quote.

Payment Information

Make check or money order payable in U.S. funds to the Association of Research Libraries, Federal ID #52-0784198-N. MasterCard and Visa accepted.

Send orders to: ARL Publications Distribution Center, P.O. Box 531, Annapolis Junction, MD 20701-0531
phone (301) 362-8196; fax (301) 206-9789; e-mail pubs@arl.org

Order online at: http://www.arl.org/pubscat/index.html